Dedication

To those (like me) who carry Christmas
in their hearts year-round and have extended a
perennial Advent. To pastors, church greeters, and
regular worshipping communities who
welcome visitors "home" for Christmas, and
to every reader of this book, that you will
never lose faith amid the festivity!

Also by Father Bill Quinlivan

Made to Praise Him: Finding My Song invites you into the adventures of a Catholic priest discovering his calling and the mysterious ways God uses our main interests/passions within a vocation to further His kingdom while enriching our lives. As well as preaching the Gospel of Jesus, every priest is encouraged to write his own gospel. This is precisely what Fr. Bill has done in his precious book *Made to Praise Him* in which he covers a vast multitude of situations in his pastoral ministry. It makes compelling reading and will nourish the spirit of anyone who takes it up.

~ Fr. Kevin Scallon, CM

I have read Fr. Bill's book *Made to Praise Him* and have laughed and smiled all the way through. It is the tender narrative of a wise and good priest and will uplift the spirit of everyone who reads it. I recommend it highly.

~ Sr. Briege McKenna, OSC

Table of Contents

Prologue

The concept of coming home is familiar, comforting, and appealing to anyone who has lived in a house filled with love. That was my experience growing up, and those blessings have taught me to value my own homecomings as well as those of loved ones. ***Coming Home to Christmas (Through Advent)*** seems like the natural follow-up to my autobiography and vocation story ***Made to Praise Him: Finding My Song.*** Play me a carol, plug in the decorations, light the wreath of anticipation, and I am instantly home! Like the proverbial fish to water and the penguin to ice is Fr. Bill Quinlivan to Christmas!

Writing these reflections for the seasons of Advent and Christmas was very similar to the process I've enjoyed when recording Christmas albums: the writing, editing and preparation begin and continue through the months of a year when *almost no one* thinks Christmas. Except authors of Christmas books and those who record music with a holiday theme. And those who, like me, find great joy and refreshment in celebrating the season ever-green, that is all year!

My prayer for those who read this work is that you deepen your spiritual connection to the Lord Jesus in His incarnation. I hope that the Spirit both sacred and mirth-filled brings you to being "at home" with what Christ offers us each Christmas—yet another opportunity to grow in His grace and to live His Gospel.

A section of prayers has been included between the early (Advent) chapters and the sleigh bell/church bell ringing (Christmas) second part. Praying through the busy and festive time from Advent to Christmas can only make everyone more at home with each other as Christ makes His home in us.

Blessed Advent, then… Merry Christmas. But as we share them both, let us pray… and now, I'll let you read!

Fr. Bill

I. ADVENT CHAPTERS

A Wreath Carol

The prayers and spirit of Advent seem to have inspired many hymn and song-writers. In the published missalettes, however, the pages for Advent are far out-numbered by Christmas. Oh, I get it---in fact, in my childhood I can recall singing *O Come, O Come Emmanuel* while secretly hoping that singing it might make Christmas come sooner, like.. now!

As my love for Advent gradually grew, and songwriting became something I found myself doing, I started to feel sympathy for the Advent hymns and carols. Perhaps the same way some people purposely adopt the runt of the litter when they choose a pet. Or they could be similarly sympathetic to Tiny Tim in *A Christmas Carol*. I see now from nearly sixty Advents and Christmases that pity slowly became awe and I have been blessed with an enriched prayer life in this annual season of anticipation. It's as if the Lord were teaching me a course in the joy of preparation, enough to earn a bachelor's degree in spiritual patience.

The symbol of the Advent wreath has always seemed to be a visual way to mark the weeks, and both religious education catechists and Catholic parochial school teachers know this. In fact, the drawing or making of an Advent wreath can be a useful art project, especially with kids who, like me, were influenced by a society that taught us Christmas comes immediately after Thanksgiving. Like that board game *Sorry*: "Sorry, Advent, we're going to ***sliiiiiiiide*** right to Christmas Eve!" Of course, that robs us of the proper time to prepare.

My composition of the *Advent Wreath Carol* came about while trying to enter into the season one year as an adult, actually as a priest who has to preach about Advent and shepherd people through this special and easily-overlooked season. It hit me one day that I could not think of a song or hymn to accompany the lighting of the candles on the wreath. Rituals seem to be augmented and up-lifted by music, so I set out to write four rather short verses, one for each candle on the wreath.

Come, O light of Jesus, let this candle show
Our holy expectation, so as we wait, we grow
Toward the day of your arrival, let your glory stir within
Until your final coming…come save us from our sin!

The beauty of the season includes the notion that it becomes a journey of prayerful waiting. For me, the experience of lighting the first purple/violet candle has always felt like ignition, the key turned and the motor starting to run. But then Advent has never been meant intended as a liturgical NASCAR race to December 25th. In my lifetime alone, it seems that the culture's need for speed has endangered a holy Advent if we get caught in that trap. Indeed, it often feels as though we board a vehicle that we are consciously having to down-shift or even put into neutral gear so as not to become a runaway train. The Polar Express may be the fastest way to the North Pole without flying reindeer, but an Advent Express or worse, un-expressed Advent denies us something important to the spiritual journey.

Advent and Christmas are celebrated at the beginning of winter, at the pivotal moment of change, connected to the concept of "shortest day of the year," as regards sunlight. An alternate expression would be the longest night, a perfect setting for light to dawn and grow. Astronomers call it the winter solstice, which occurs in the Northern Hemisphere on or about December 21st. In the Southern Hemisphere it happens around June 21, so that might be where the tradition of hanging Christmas trees upside-down comes from. (Just kidding… If you're reading this in the Southern Hemisphere, invite me to do a concert and explain this hemisphere thing regarding Advent/Christmas!)

So each verse begins "Come O Light of Jesus," not an original concept of mine but a traditional and scriptural reference (John 8:12) to our Lord and Savior. In deepest darkness, there's a common human desire for light. The light/darkness contrast can illustrate the struggle of human hearts with dark places inside of us. As wax candles burn, especially if we light them numerous times over the days of

Advent, the wick burns down and it becomes difficult to see the flame or light. Doesn't that somehow represent our need to let Christ's saving light burn down deep into our being?

The last line of the first verse "come save us from our sin" gives, of course, religious and Christian meaning to the coming Messiah. For Catholics, we have the opportunity to seek the forgiveness and mercy of the Lord in the sacrament of Reconciliation or Penance. Most parishes offer a special time of communal prayer for repentance in an Advent Penance Service, followed by opportunities for individuals to go to Confession. Personally, I have always loved Advent Penance services. Somewhere in my upbringing, the tidying up and cleaning the house for Christmas has always called for a parallel interior house-keeping experience.

The second verse of my Advent Wreath hymn attempts to express that:

Come, O Light of Jesus, every waiting hour
Calls us to repentance, your manifested power
May this second candle increase each heart's desire
To live a holy Advent, illumined by your fire.

One year after the release of my *Blanket of Stars* CD, aware of the brief window of opportunity to market and share Advent-Christmas music, I decided to produce a music video. The studio where I had recorded the album had two bright, talented young women in residence for the summer producing some other video projects. So they agreed to tackle my first music video. We shot it on a very hot August day, and had to stir all our imaginative powers to think Advent. I was wearing a winter-weight purple vestment, and we hoisted the large Advent Wreath from the basement of Blessed Sacrament Parish for an off-season appearance. I'm very pleased with the end product; it is my most-viewed video on YouTube, currently at over 10,000 viewings.

The visual for the second verse includes a scene of a young man, a teen, entering a church and seeing a poster for an Advent Penance Service. He comes in to pray, then notices that the light is on over the confessional, so he comes in. We found a natural talent in Robert Fera, Jr. Before his filmed "confession," he has a look of serious self-examination and just a bit of conscience-pinched discomfort. But after I "gave absolution" and blessed him, he is seen coming back into church with a great smile on his face.

My Pastoral Associate at the time, Sr. Lucette Kinecki, CSSF and I have had annual friendly debates about Advent wreath candle care. Should the wax be trimmed so as to let the flame be seen throughout the church? Is it best to let the candles burn naturally, even if the flame goes out of sight? Would oil candles be more efficient, though we lose the visual effect of a pillar burning down over the four weeks? Would it be better to invest in brass followers, the round candle-top devices that help ease the wax downward in an even manner? Then there's the question of the order in which to light them, and the placement of the rose candle. And how simple should the wreath be—augmented with purple and pink ribbons? Kept simple for a desert feel?

One thing is certain. When planning to shoot the video for the Advent Wreath Hymn, I really wanted Sr. Lucette to be part of the third verse:

Come O light of Jesus, anticipation sings
The shade of rose, rejoicing, our preparation brings
Ignite within all children your gift of flickering joy
And deepen earth's awareness of Divinity's infant boy.

Sr. Lucette's religious name is in honor of her mother, a

sweet lady whose name was Lucy. And St. Lucy's name means light. The combination of the light of a third candle and the joy of the rose-colored turn-the-corner feel of Gaudete Sunday made Sr. Lucette the obvious choice to enact common Advent tasks. In the video, she's in a kitchen rolling out dough and baking Christmas cookies, her lovely smiling face making you want to put on an apron, grab a rolling pin and join her. Then, she places a cookie sheet full of cut-outs in the oven, sits and opens her breviary. It's quite a nice scene, directed by Rebekah Palowski for Quiet Waters Productions. My favorite part, however, is the shameless commercial for my Christmas CD, when, before she sits to pray, she hits the pause button on a CD player and removes my *Blanket of Stars* CD, ever-so-subtly showing the album art to the camera before beginning her prayer.

The fourth verse includes a key change, meant to indicate the growing joy and anticipation of Christmas. All of it is written in minor keys, for those chords have a sound and air of mystery to them, unlike major chords and keys. As Advent brings us to the major event of Christ's Incarnation, our status of being "minor" or like little children draws us into the wonder of it all. It's major!

Come, O Light of Jesus,
all creation held its breath
Love's mystery incarnate came
to take our sin and death
With new hope for salvation,
we light the wreath around
Like Heaven's smile still shining,
your promised Peace profound.

In the early scenes of the video where I'm singing next to the wreath, we used dry ice to create a cloudy mist. In a few of the out-takes, the fog was so thick that when I pronounced a word beginning with a "p", the smoke went flying away like I was exhaling a giant Advent cigarette. Having been a bingo worker from my youth, I knew that cloud and the stench it brought into hair and clothing. But never being a smoker, this puff-the-magic-priest effect had to be cut out. But it provided lots of laughter in the midst of a long day of shooting the video.

Actually, one can draw a connection between the clouds of smoke/mist around the wreath and the final scene of the song's music video. We accompany the fourth verse by gathering everyone who was in the first three scenes into a small country church called Epiphany of Our Lord in Langford, New York. The camera was set up just outside the front door of the church, and by this time it was a summer night! Shooting in toward the sanctuary, the people entering appeared in silhouette. I credit that to Rebekah and her assistant, Sara's artistic gifts.

The story line for the final verse leads to a time of Eucharistic Adoration. Instead of clouds of dry ice, I am now shown incensing the Blessed Sacrament. The church of the Epiphany has large statues of the Magi, carefully placed around the sanctuary. The dome above is painted like a night sky with the star of Bethlehem in view. Fittingly, as my *Advent Wreath Carol* is playing over the video, we were actually singing the "O come let us adore Him" refrain of *Adeste Fideles.* I often use that throughout the year at adoration services because it has become so deeply ingrained in the memories of people.

A tag line for the song is simply:

Come, O Light O Jesus, Maranatha, Jesus... Come!

The word Maranatha has two meanings, according to my research. Because New Testament Greek did not put space between words, it can either mean *Marana tha* as two words or Maranatha as one. The meanings: "Our Lord Come!" or "Our Lord has come! "To me this has a profound Advent meaning, especially in the context of adoration of the Most Blessed Sacrament. As Catholics, we believe that Our Lord has come and remains truly present in the Eucharist. Thus, we adore Him in person.

At the same time, the first two weeks of Advent have a focus more on the Second Coming or glorious return of Jesus at the end of time. It helps us segue from the Solemnity of Christ the King at the end of Ordinary Time into Advent. The coming Lord is already present, but with every Advent, and every Christmas, we still await His final coming.

The last shot of the video includes the camera panning up, after I have given the congregation a Eucharistic blessing/ benediction. As the song ends and the word "come" echoes and fades, we look up to the star of Bethlehem, and at the same time can recall the disciples at Christ's Ascension looking intently at the sky.

Make A Little Room

Things are getting just a little crowded,
Our town is getting just a little tight...
The world is getting just a little crazy—
I don't know anyone who could not appreciate
Just a silent night....

How do you rein in a runaway reindeer? Let's not even consider the flying type. The culture of hustle and bustle and the hurried, frenetic pace of the so-called "Christmas Shopping Season" can run over our attempts to live the Advent time of preparation. And for our efforts to be prayerful, careful, and to move slowly, in many ways we might very well find hoof or boot-marks on our foreheads. But let that not dissuade us. All the hype cannot buy time or make it go faster. About four weeks, depending on where December 25th lands, is what we all get. What we choose to do with it is really in our hands. Mostly...or is it partly? Or some years, hardly?

Throughout these reflections you will hear me preaching Advent like a reformed smoker, a sober drinker, or that person who has been involved in the latest parish renewal program and is now determined to convince you how much your life would eternally benefit from the same thing. I have come to a point where I love Advent almost as much as Christmas, but I believe that we each need to find our own affection for the weeks leading up to Christmas.

Before I go any further, let me say: *My name is Fr. Bill Quinlivan and I am a reformed Advent Accelerator!* Yes, I have experienced full-speed-ahead, pedal-to-the-floor races in the extreme sport of Advent Aversion or Christmas Crush. Happily, I have come a long way, thank God. With the support of my church and its holy, higher (actually, ***highest)*** power! this brief season of waiting that flies in the face of…flying in the face of Christmas, my experience has mellowed me.

Again in the interests of full disclosure, I have discovered a loop-hole that keeps me somewhat balanced in the ongoing conversations/arguments about a spiritually proper Advent followed by a joyous, holy Christmas. After my journey of conversion, I can attest that every year, even with a full four-week Advent, my shopping, decorating, and writing Christmas cards do get finished by Christmas Eve's first verse of *O Come All Ye Faithful*. But there is a little secret I need to share; perhaps it can help you or a family member keep their Christmas-mania more under control.

It's music. Since about the sixth grade, when I first joined a church choir, I discovered that the rehearsals for Christmas allow you *legally* to sing carols and songs of that season long before the first candle of Advent is even purchased. As early as October, in some cases, and then all through November! And it has been a saving grace for me, but it's best kept behind the doors of music ministry rehearsal spaces. And, for study purposes only… played in my stereo headphones.

While in seminary, Christmas music toward the end of the Fall semester was like prescribed medication for stress relief while writing research papers and studying for final exams. As it has always been a "happy place" as some say, for my heart and soul, I publicly confess that under my headphones on hot Summer days, I may even take a brief, mentally cooling trip into Christmas music. But again, under the rationalization that I'm learning *new* songs for upcoming Christmas concerts in December. I learn best by repetition. Song selection, in my head, sometimes begins before the first leaves change color, of course only for the sake of my being properly prepared. And, okay…yes…I admit it gives me a thrill to hear it in Summer. But I'm trying to explain that off-season listening can be very practical for ministry purposes. Uh-huh. Are you buying this explanation?

Make a Little Room, clear a little space
Stop before you push someone right through the season
Make a Little Room, let a person through
Won't somebody Make a Little Room?

One early December day during my seminary years, a fellow student saw me hanging some lights around my doorway and confronted me with the accusation that I was "Ruining everybody's Advent!" My…such drama. I suggested that my heart was contemplating the season of waiting while I decorated, and that his emotional outburst indicated perhaps a need for a little quiet time. Then, as the part of me that has my mother's gumption, simply said: "Nobody's forcing you to come to my room. Good bye!"

The more I reflect upon this, within the celebration of the liturgies of Advent even I will not let a bit of Christmas slip in. But my private living quarters and car's CD player are actually part of a gigantic choir room. In other words, yes. Christmas music is played- but always outside of Advent Masses.

The inspiration for *Make A Little Room* came several years later. After ordination, immersed in full-time church ministry as a parish priest, I discovered that the madness of "Black Friday" shopping the morning after Thanksgiving had an evil twin that appeared just before the Christmas Eve 4:00 PM vigil Mass.

Assigned to the largest suburban parish in the Buffalo diocese, I was given the duty to preside at the first Christmas Mass. "I've been preparing for this ***since August***!" I secretly whispered to myself with glee. As I neared the sacristy, I heard a din. Coming closer, it became a loud, boisterous noise as if Macy's had opened a new location in the pews of St. Gregory the Great parish, and someone just announced that the people who spoke the loudest would win a free Cabbage Patch Doll!

St. Gregory's celebrates three simultaneous 4:00 Masses, because the "overflow" crowds also flow over (and make more over-flow) in the school gym and a large parish center. I discovered that people arrive about ninety minutes early to seek a parking spot. And then they shop for a pew. I was honestly horrified to see a number of people carrying coffee cups into church, sitting and reading novels and shouting greetings across the crowd of hundreds who gathered over an hour before Mass began.

The following year, I came up with a plan. I may have even considered it a pastoral duty to listen to Christmas music in July that year to be sure to tackle the issue with enough holly in my heart. I decided to arrive early myself, stand at the podium, and welcome people, then lead them in some "choir practice" of a few carols. Gently offering repeated reminders that we were in sacred space, that Advent wasn't officially over until 4:00 PM, I had a Santa's sack full of focusing exercises.

Did it work? Well…have you ever had the experience of trying to clear a sidewalk during a ferocious snowstorm? You scoop up a couple of inches of the white stuff and a moment later it looks as if you didn't start yet. We call it frustration.

But it's better than running back to the rectory to put my Amy Grant Christmas CDs on full-blast. There were some who apparently got it… and then they heard a message rather pointedly based on my experiences in the homily, and the new song, *Make A Little Room.*

The family's so frantic about Christmas
We hardly even stop to see the lights
Activities like shopping for the gift list,
They wrap us up in over-do
And parents look relieved it's through
December 25th at night…

Advent's days offer a terrific opportunity sincerely to make room for God in our lives. A section of this book includes some specially-written prayers to assist the reader in that attempt. And like all conversion, it happens in steps. Often, small steps…but then, if we're heading in the right direction to celebrate them. You may have a long-held desire to spend extra time in church in December, but find yourself frustrated by other realities and duties at this time in your life. It's okay. We can savor Advent in the every-day.

I've composed prayers to use before house decorating, one in anticipation of baking Christmas cookies, and even a gift-wrapping prayer. I've also included rosary meditations called the Advent Mysteries of the Rosary. If we compartmentalize those pre-Christmas activities too much and see them as separate/distant from our spiritual life, we can easily end up feeling guilty when Christmas arrives as if we purposely short-circuited Advent. Instead, why not inject the work and fun of the season with prayerful awareness of our Lord who makes all things new, holy and profound while we stay connected in heart and mind to His presence.

I wonder if it's worth my while to mention
The coming of our Savior as a boy.
Hey, let's give Jesus all of our attention!
His message, His nativity says:
"Say an Advent prayer with me"
Busy, dizzy people...

Make a little room, You're too close, too loud
Where's the joy of Christmas in this kind of season?
Make a Little Room, maybe use a plow...
Won't somebody Make a little room?

In the final verse of this song, the refrain returns to the notion of "clear a little space" by my purposely not singing a few of the phrases. Literally, there is a vocal-free phrase or two, applying what the whole idea promotes. It's either very freeing or distracting for the listener. Some think: "He forgot the words to his own song—again? Did anyone listen closely to this recording before they sent it to the duplicator??" And others, I hope, say: "Oh, now I get it-the silence makes room in the song." As we say in Catholic parish centers...Bingo!

Still others just listen in Advent silence without a whole lot of analysis. And it becomes prayer.

Listen

Listen in the waiting, watch the night grow dark
Believers become beacons to spread the Spirit's spark
All our Advent songings cry for Christ's pure light
Our deepest well of longings bemoan un-focused sight

Listen in the winter, put plans to hibernate
Receive bouquets of quiet, let rest regenerate
Seek joy in contemplation, like bundled kids love snow
Sip time alone with Jesus, watch grace in your life grow

Will the Lord speak?
Will you let Him?
His abiding grace will suffice…
All too often we live like we forget
that God is with us… Jesus Christ!

Listen in the forest, footsteps in the wild
Alone in nature's splendor, be simple as a child
Footprints in snowy carpet, heavenly scent of pine
A doe observes your yearning for streams of love divine

Will the Lord speak? Will you let Him?
His abiding grace will suffice…

Listen in the waiting…
Listen in the winter…
Listen in the forest…

Listen!

others may have asked for a mirror to hold under his nose and see if he was still breathing. And by three minutes, the wrist watches were certainly checked by a number of folks. Waiting is hard and although I have never tried this method of teaching people to listen, his creativity was admirable!

I had never thought of quiet time as something that could be tied up in a bouquet like flowers, but when scribbling this lyric during prayer it occurred that the gift of quiet could please the soul as much as giving a dozen roses to one's love "just because". Listening in times of silence does actually give something to us. Unlike a priest standing wordlessly near the Advent wreath during homily time, when we consciously decide to clear away noise, we are often blessed.

Contemplation is one of those words that we who seek a deep spiritual life can find to be a great mystery. Mystics and saints might probe so deeply that it seems hard to touch to the average believer. I try to remind myself that there is joy in contemplation. In a sense, it can almost feel like as much "play" as "pray". So verse two of the song makes the comparison to bundled-up children frolicking in the snow. Consider the difference between the kids' response to a call to come inside ("Aw, can't we stay out a little longer?") to the way we sometimes approach prayer time ("How long am I going to try to do this?") and you might see my point here. Pray it, play it, and learning to listen can be a delight.

FOREST JUMP

At the risk of sounding prideful, I love the third verse of this song! As someone who grew up in a city, the sight of a deer has been quite rare. I've been blessed to be able to make a few winter retreats and days of prayer during Advent when there's snow on the ground and some woodsy area in which to walk and pray. If there isn't snow falling, I've learned that one can walk into an unknown area and later re-trace your footsteps on the way back. I've also learned that the season of joyful anticipation we call Advent over-laps with deer hunting season, so a far-away gunshot can quicken my heartbeat and my pace, even forcing me to retreat back to safety!

Being in the gaze of a deer in winter when I hike out into their domain is very different from the commonly used expression "a deer in the headlights." Unlike that stunned expression, the deer observing us in the forest offers a wonderful insight into God's creation. Deer seem to have very good hearing, which may make them good listeners. In the Scriptures, Psalm 42:1 teaches us that our longing for the Lord can be like the deer's longing for running water.

My lyric turns the tables on the forest-walking silence-seeker. The doe with its wide and gorgeous eyes comes to look at me, at you, at us. This beautiful animal that lives by instinct and nature's longings for food, shelter and water can literally stop us in our tracks. Especially if we ponder that our Advent longing, when our mind and heart's field of view is expanded in prayer, comes into the clear. Wouldn't it be wild if God gave these animals the ability to detect whether we are a people of longing?

PAGING MR. WEBSTER

One of the joys of songwriting for me is the freedom to play with words. And on occasion, I like to try to make new ones. Webster's Dictionary has become a valuable asset in writing books and bulletin columns. But I sometimes wonder if my games might give Mr. Webster a migraine headache. I never knew the chap, but in my imagination I have to believe that he would have enjoyed word play, much as a jazz musician can respect a composed melody but dance around it with creative flair.

Advent ***songings*** has become my new word for the season of waiting, praying, preparing, and longing. It actually sounds better sung… and I long to sing *Listen* again every Advent. More importantly, I need to listen to what *Listen* says, and not sing it. Where did I put my winter boots? Where's the nearest forest??

Gaudete: The Joy of Anticipation

Irony abounds in the statement "I just *can't wait* for Christmas." It's obvious that as you drive through neighborhoods in early November and see lights and inflatable lawn decorations being carefully placed for optimum effect. But we must wait for Christmas. And the season of waiting is holy Advent. If you cannot bear four weeks of Advent, then listen to this good news: YOU need it more than the rest of us! Yes you may very well be in the majority if you desire an express flight to Christmas. That doesn't make it right, nor does it add to Advent except as another time of year our high-speed culture rushes through with reckless abandon.

The real meaning of the sacred feasts calls us to be real, to slow down a bit, and digest the activities as much as the cookies and cakes. Advent seems to have become a secret, but like a recipe for your sweetest dessert that co-workers ask to copy, this season was never meant to be kept secret. I preach this as a convert to Advent, and as any conversion witness will tell you, I'm still in the process. Parish communities struggle, too. Organizations and ministries wanting to have a social or party have a tendency in some places to move them further toward the start of Advent. If you announced an Advent party, chances are many people will show up wearing those Christmas sweaters December 1st, ladies pinned with Santas and reindeer. Or you may find that people don't flock to your event at all because of its title.

FLOCK PARTY

There's a style of spraying imitation snow on trees and wreaths that they call flocking. Doing a bit of research, I found that people in certain regions of the world that are snowless have tried this for longer than we may imagine. Back in the 19th century, substances such as flour or cotton were attached to greenery to make it—what, whitery? A 1929 issue of Popular Mechanics included a recipe of varnish, corn starch and flaky material to flock. Varnish? That had to smell worse than bayberry candles.

Tree flocking hit a new stride in the 1950s and 60s when aluminum trees appeared and won the hearts of the post-WWII and baby boomer generation. Convenient, perhaps. Messy, you bet. Fake, better? I think not. But for the sake of stirring up compassion for those in sunny, dry climates, as a northeastern America person, I am really trying to cut them some slack.

My brother Joe and sister Mary were taught 5th grade by a Sister of Mercy named Sr. Mary Gaudentia. Besides being known as the little nun who could inspire her class to sell amazing amounts of Easter candy for the sake of a pizza party, she also annually explained to her class how her religious name connects to the Third Sunday of Advent. (By the way, her methods of driving up sales included homework-free nights for certain peaks in sales numbers. The result was a steady record of championship honors for chocolate sales, though it is rumored that her students may have had slightly lower SAT-Scholastic Aptitude Test scores in high school. Sometimes trade-offs, when connected to free pizza in grammar school make sense.)

Gaudete (pronounced Gow-DAY-tay) is the Latin word from which Sr. Mary Gaudentia received her name. It means rejoice, which comes from St. Paul's letter to the Philippians 4:4-5: "Rejoice in the Lord always, again I say rejoice. Let your forbearance be known to all, for the Lord is near at hand; have no anxiety about anything, but in all things, by prayer and supplication, with thanksgiving, let your requests be known to God."

Advent historically originated as forty days of fasting and prayer in preparation for Christmas, beginning on the feast of St. Martin, November 11th. (This might explain my Advent-Christmas attachment, since I was born November 12th... Or I may just be reading into it. Please, let me have my fun.) In the 9th century, Advent was reduced to four weeks so as to differentiate it from Lent. It's still supposed to have a penitential nature. It's often hard to tell that from Catholic homes festooned with giant, waving Disney characters and loud speakers blasting pre-recorded Christmas songs eighteen hours a day. Unless, seeing that, we are inspired to pray: Lord have mercy on us all, forgive us for we know not what we do.

The sense of Advent's theological themes of expectation and waiting have two streams of focus; the first two weeks of waiting really emphasize the Second Coming of Christ. Gaudete Sunday signals a time of rejoicing because the feast of Christ's first arrival is nearing. In a sense, it shifts the church from "repent/convert and get ready, for He will return" mode to "let's experience the joy of conversion, for Christmas is coming." For that reason my preference for choosing a date of parish Penance Services has often been near Gaudete Sunday. A good confession really can be much more important than the best swig of eggnog at your office "holiday party." And the verse in Philippians about having no anxiety does not refer to whether or not our shopping will be done in time, but more about our soul being cleansed and freed to proclaim fully the joy of Jesus' birth.

Lyrics from my songs act much like my homilies, as I attempt to express a message that I usually need to hear myself as much as the intended audience/congregation does. One hot summer day, when needing to ponder Advent or Christmas so as not to let high humidity kill any trace of humility in my soul, I wrote the follow song:

GAUDETE (ANTICIPATING CHRISTMAS DAY)

Don't lose the Christmas tree in decorations
Don't burden all the branches with lights
Hold back just a little with your tinsel
And adorn your soul with Christmas white!
Don't try to force your friends to drink egg nog
Don't push George Bailey to the brink
Make time to pray in days of Advent
Soak your to-do list in God's sink

Frost your cookie-cut hopes with some Gaudete
Hear the promise in the prophets
Everything they say
When we're yearning for Jesus in a profound way
We grow holy
Anticipating Christmas Day!

Do discover waiting this December
Pause and ponder mysteries divine
Rejoicing, light the candle that is rosy
The dawning of our Christ is such a hopeful sign!
Let God be there in all your preparations
Sing "Come, Emmanuel" a brighter way

No sale compares to saving done by Jesus
The reason in your season brings His peace to stay..

Frost your cookie-cut hopes with some Gaudete….

FROSTING, NOT FLOCKING

Some bakers refer to it as icing, but in our family it's always been called frosting. Mom's recipe was simply one she found on the side of a box of confectioner's sugar. Like her recipe for chocolate fudge, the frosting also included some vanilla. I'm not sure where my mother's recipe for Christmas cookies originated, but it has remained for almost sixty years a part of my immediate family's sweet treats for the holiday.

It's a recipe for cut-outs, and one that the most health-conscious person would probably reject if he/she ever read the ingredients. Lard, buttermilk, sugar, milk, flour, and eggs. The cookies come out flaky like piecrust, so they need the assistance of frosting to complete the wonderful recipe. Though an occasional visitor might announce with great pride: "I don't need frosting on a cookie..." I have to disagree with this theory. They are incredible, edible, and I'd venture to say heavenly.

The lyric above says, "don't force your friends to drink egg nog. Don't push George Bailey to the brink." It's funny how people have their favorite foods of the season, and the debate about fruitcake has undoubtedly been the subject of countless stand-up comedy routines. My family never discussed it at all, for no cake of fruit and rum ever crossed our doorway.

Gaudete Sunday is the frosting on the cookie, a brief outburst of joy. The liturgical color for that day creates another conversation among clergy. It's called rose, but many of those who make vestments tend to choose fabric that has a closer resemblance to a bright pink medication that one takes for digestive issues. My friends at Buffalo's St. Luke's Mission of Mercy were given a vestment for Gaudete Sunday that has to be the pinkest and glossiest thing this side of Las Vegas' Liberace Museum! I like to say that it takes a lot of love and devotion for a priest to wear either rose or hot pink. And I joke that cell phones and cameras are strictly forbidden during the Third Sunday of Advent!

Jumping John

At the beginning of the gospel of Luke, a priest named Zechariah, the husband of Elizabeth, went into the sanctuary to burn incense. The angel of the Lord appeared to him, and seeing that he was troubled, said, "Do not be afraid." The message said that their prayer to have a son had been answered, that they would "have joy and gladness and many would rejoice at his birth." (Luke 1:14, New American Bible) Then comes an exciting detail: "He will be filled with the Holy Spirit even from his mother's womb."

After the angel Gabriel came to tell Mary that she would bear God's only Son, she headed out to visit her kinswoman Elizabeth. And verse 1:41 says "When Elizabeth heard the sound of Mary's greeting, the infant leaped in her womb." Of course, six months into a pregnancy, a growing baby would begin to move and kick. But this child was filled with the Spirit, so to my mind it was more of a dance.

Jump for joy, leap for love
Live with eyes fixed above
Do a jig like John
When Jesus came
and then gracefully
his life and Gospel you'll proclaim!

Filled with the Spirit all souls can dance
like the tiny Baptist in his mother's womb.
A joyous celebration at the slightest glance;
there's no hesitation
in the Lord's ballroom!

The common expression a "leap of faith" took on new meaning when Elizabeth's child was still forming inside of her. Did his mother's heart start to pound, sending a signal to the infant like a blast of music that calls dancers out onto the floor? Was little Johnny B. Baptist skipping rope with the umbilical cord?

One never knows where the Spirit of God will take a body when it's filled with sweet inspiration!

Advent is one of the church's seasons where the Baptist appears. His wordless leaping seems to illustrate the joy of the season of anticipation. It sings of Israel's hope and years of waiting coming to a turning point. The same Holy Spirit that would later give John a "fire" for calling people to repent and turn from sin first comes to ignite a flame in him before he's even breathing on his own. We might even say that the Virgin Mary who had just experienced the Holy Spirit coming upon her at the Annunciation and "overshadowing" her, brought the Spirit's fullness and shared it.

Have you ever been at an event where music and a dance floor accompany the expectation that people will dance? Sometimes, there is much hesitation. It can stem from self-consciousness, being insecure of one's ability to move to the beat. But John the Baptist's prophetic ballet of sorts was purely uninhibited. How could he have known whether he would be considered a good dancer? We don't even know if there was music, but I'd imagine that his momma's beating heart and a little adrenaline in the bloodstream would set him moving pretty freely.

When you meet someone with a "different drum"
say a prayer your visit helps them hear God's band
Gather two or more in the good Lord's name
Soon, you're marching off to Zion

with new friends at hand!
Jump for joy... leap for love...

In a musical ensemble, when one person plays an instrument or sings out of synchronization with the tempo set by the leader, it can really stand out. And the best musical directors can convince that person that (sometimes, after several attempts to help one find the right rhythm) the role of equipment manager still allows one to have their name in the program for a performance.

Jesus would come across many people who, as the cliché goes, "march to their own drummer." His presence, His merciful patience and ability to breathe peace into a troubled heart can solve many such tempo disorders. In the extreme, His exorcism of demons would have spiritually silenced the banging drum of the evil one whose tricks discourage us from fearlessly following Christ.

The phrase "do not be afraid" was spoken countless times in His ministry.

If you move in sync with His perfect will
You get a taste of life fantastic as it's planned for you
With King David's zeal, with abandon free
You can cast away a counting of one-two-, one-two...
Jump for joy, leap for love...

Israel's King David was not only a regal figure but a musician who played the harp and composed psalms to glorify God. And he also danced! 2 Samuel 6:14 says: "Then David, girt with a linen apron, came dancing before the Lord with abandon as he and all the Israelites were bringing the ark with shouts of joy and the sound of the horn." (NAB) Before the presence of the Lord, with abandon, sounds like an ancestor of Jumping Johnny to me!

Often on dance floors at weddings, there are certain group dances that people try to do together. The Electric Slide and the Macarena can encourage the shy type to get off their chairs and follow someone's direction. Repetitive steps make it look easy. In generations gone by there were dances like the Lindy Hop, Charleston, Jitterbug, Twist, Loco-Motion and Watusi. Many of them have specific songs that encourage people to join in.

I cannot picture John the Baptist at a wedding reception. He was living in the desert by the time he reached the age where he might be invited. And the caterers would have been insulted if he ordered a special diet of grasshoppers and wild honey. No, the Baptist's dance beat was deep within him and abandoning himself to the Holy Spirit it made him unique. In fact, Jesus calls him the greatest of all the prophets.

Days come when all of us would rather sit
and watch the Fred and Ginger types perform
But this dance is not a show
it's a holy way to Heaven's Joy—
so why say no??
Jump for Joy…

When I attend a function and for some reason do not participate in the dancing, it feels as though I missed part of it. For me, the conditions have to be right. The music has to move me, and group dances with set choreography bore me, to be honest. Lighting is best dimmed, and please, no mirrors on the walls! I also prefer that no one videotape the dancing. And then… when the Spirit moves me. Abandon and jumping for joy follow, like David before the Ark and Jumping Johnny, aka, St. John the Baptist.

Here Is Your God

The people who walked in darkness
are healed in great light
Finding Peace in the Advent of Jesus
with a word, he turns us back to right
Only fools wrap a present that's broken
or mail a gift card whose total is spent
Now's the time to prepare and repair things
Bring ourselves to the Lord and repent!
No, we're not deserving- we're too quick to make excuse
Humbly come to the God that you're serving
He gave power to bind and loose…

In the desert, prepare the way for the Lord
He makes straight in the wasteland a highway
the valleys filled, and every hill will be made low.
HERE IS YOUR GOD…
so approach and let His Mercy flow!

In the hand of the Lord, your good God
you shall be like a glorious crown
They will not ever call you" forsaken"
He says "You're my delight.." smiling down
We're affecting the whole world's salvation
if forgiveness is something we learn
Come like prodigal people, expectant
See your bridegroom, rejoice as you turn!
It's not about seeking perfection
How can sand stay secure in a sieve?

Holy grace resurrects fallen nature
Then it calls us to go, and forgive!

In the desert, prepare the way of the Lord…
HERE IS YOUR GOD! So approach…
and let His mercy flow!

The person and prophecy of St. John the Baptist are so important that by the time Jesus begins his own public ministry he takes up John's motto: "Repent! The Kingdom of God is at hand!" In this vein, the Baptist's presence in Lent where repentance has a more urgent call also fits into Advent. Preparation, anticipation, waiting and listening in the weeks before Christmas can also call us to make a good examination of conscience.

I've presided at several healing Masses in early December. At least one year at Blessed Sacrament Parish in Tonawanda we offered prayer to heal families. This included living and deceased, and was an invitation to find peace with old hurts and wounds as part of our preparation for Christmas. The fairy tale approach to family gatherings seems always to lead to disappointment and even fractured hearts. But standing before God, aware of how our broken humanity affects our behavior, even (and especially!) those to whom we're closest.

"Healed in great light" is one of my lyrical twists on the Scripture passage that says "walked in great light." I'd like to think that my own awareness of my shortcomings in relationships –even the one with God Himself- finds me inviting others to pray for healing. That would include me praying for the same light, not just as intercessor but also as a fellow pilgrim.

"Only fools wrap a present that's broken, or mail a gift card whose total is spent…" Does this not acknowledge that our hyperactive pre-Christmas busy lives bring us exhausted and rather full of self-pity to family gatherings to or Mass to celebrate the feast of joy? It reminds me of people who announce to someone who moves into their home: "***Don't*** talk to me until I've had my first cup of coffee!" To that, I say; get a coffee maker for your room and don't come out until you're going to be nice!

ABUNDANT JOY, GREAT REJOICING

In Isaiah 9:2 and following, the people who walk in darkness and see a great light are also promised "abundant joy and great rejoicing," where burdens are smashed. To me, an Advent Penance service provides the perfect opportunity to bring and name our burdens and give them to Christ to smash! *Here Is your God* was written for an Advent night of Confessions. To those who feel isolated and distant from others, who find themselves asking, "Where is God in all of this?" my answer is that He comes face to face with us when we humble ourselves and admit the need to be forgiven and healed.

Chapter 40 of Isaiah, verses 3-5 have that John the Baptist flavor:

> "*A voice cries out: In the desert prepare the way of the Lord! Make straight in the wasteland a highway for our God! Every valley shall be filled in, every mountain and hill shall be made low; the rugged land shall be made a plain, the rough country, a broad valley. Then the glory of the Lord shall be revealed...*"

The human soul has a landscape that can include valleys, hills, mountains, and plains. Our emotional well-being, our ability to seek and keep deepening our faith life, during chapters of our life that are much more like desert than stream, can be difficult if not discouraging. What do we expect when we approach a priest for the Sacrament of Reconciliation? Advent's expectation theme goes way beyond the trite "shopping list" of what we think we need, the wants and desires that can often lead to dead ends.

Here, in the present moment, we all need to stop the roller coaster of Christmas preparations that can make us forget the true meaning of what we prepare to celebrate. The second verse of this song might surprise you because another section of Isaiah's prophecy has a word that often catches us off guard.

The first reading for the Vigil of Christmas (statistically, the best-attended liturgy in any parish where I've been assigned) hears this proclaimed:

"For Zion's sake I will not be silent.
For Jerusalem's sake I will not be quiet,
until her vindication shines forth like the dawn
and her victory like a burning torch...
You shall be called by
a new name pronounced by the mouth of the Lord.
You shall be a glorious crown in the hand of the Lord...
you shall be called 'my delight.' "

For our sake, I've used these words as an Advent refection because the physical, emotional reality of the shape people find themselves in after finding a pew at Christmas Eve Mass might not be so glorious, so delightful. Yet this is such good news, with so much promise. The Lord speaks boldly through his prophet to be heard, and He will not be silent. Perhaps so few of our moments pre-Christmas and late-Advent are silent unless we wrestle the clock and calendar into submission!

When we invest some time in examination of conscience and receive the grace of God's forgiveness, aren't we tapping into the flow of what Christ came here to accomplish? Nobody would have thought to kneel next to the manger and whisper a request to the newborn baby Jesus. The risen one, the glorious victor over sin is here making himself available, as he waits.

When we realize that "Here is my God," we can experience His response: "Here is my delight..." Remember, our sins and weaknesses do not surprise Him. It's already known in full. But people who admit the times they freely chose to walk in darkness can be bathed in the light that saves, forgives, and heals.

Then, we come through Advent toward Christmas with a gift of our renewed self to offer to the Lord a heart open for praise, a reconciled valley-filled, mountain-leveled disciple eager to share the peace that only Jesus can give. So, approach... and let His mercy flow!

Nicholas: More Or Less?

My appreciation of St. Nicholas came late. Probably forty years late. In my childhood, Christmas themes included only Jesus Christ's birth and the Santa Claus narrative. And honestly not in that order until some growing up occurred! The process of maturing has absolutely put Jesus first where He belongs. And that thought has become a strong under-current in much of my Advent and Christmas seasons as a priest. I've been a die-hard Santa fan, so I understand the ho-ho-hold that this famous man in red has had on many people/families.

My friend Fr. Ray Donohue grew up in a house across the street from ours. He and his father could have been department store window display designers. I know that his dad, Joe, washed windows in a long-gone downtown Buffalo department store called Flint and Kent's. Perhaps that is where their art of professional Christmas decorating came from, although department stores don't wash their windows in Buffalo in December or they end up adding "a delightful coating of ice" to the window decoration scheme.

Before Thanksgiving dinner's dessert came anywhere near digestion, the Donohues began hanging Christmas lights around their front hall windows. I would be green with envy, and also delighted to see that taking place, for any hint of Christmas was a thrill to this kid. Even though my parents' annual response to seeing it was "No, Bill. It's too soon to decorate. Let's wait until at least December 15th."

One year, I invited my mother to come across the street to Donohues with me to see the mantle displays, the rotating aluminum tree and elaborate garlands over doorways. She was notably impressed, but on the way back across the street she uttered the Kass Quinlivan version of what Ralphie, the kid in *A Christmas Story*, hears when he asks for a Red Ryder bb gun: "You'll shoot your eye out!" My mother's declarative sentence was not so violent but just as determined: "Too many Santa Clauses!"

This, of course, led to an informal Santa-count when our decorations finally were freed from the boxes in the attic. We certainly had only a fraction of the Donohues' collection of jolly old elves, but then we also had only about one fifth of their total decoration inventory. And this was decades prior to the introduction of those storage rental units people get for the safe keeping of their excess "stuff." (Secretly, I consoled myself with the thought that onc day I would have my own home, and decorate as much as I pleased. The boxes of un-used decorations currently crowding my rectory basement are evidence that I followed through in that foolishness.)

I'm convinced that Mom's "too many Santa Clauses" conclusion was part of her desire to make sure that our Christmas was centered on the birth of the Savior. But decades later, since I discovered St. Nicholas, the true and not-meant-to-be secret identity of Mr. Claus, I wish now that I could time travel back to 1970 to make a case for December 6th to begin decorating. After all, it's a saint's feast day! There's Jesus all over that, right?

HOLY, GOOD ST. NICHOLAS

Holy, good Saint Nicholas, posters we will paint
Got to tell the whole wide world
That you are a saint
As a bishop, in your life,
Wonders never ceased
From your childhood
Jesus called you to be a priest!

Holy, good Saint Nicholas,
Christmas makes us pause
Will we see you at the mall,
Dressed as Santa Claus?
Is not love the perfect gift
Jesus gives for free
So who needs computer games in eternity?

Holy, good St. Nicholas, how you intercede
Praying for the little ones
Children all in need
When we give with generous hearts
All the poor are blessed
We love you, St. Nicholas
We think you're the best!

SAINT AND SANTA, THE SAME GUY!

My Byzantine priest friend Fr. Joseph Bertha inspired my deeper appreciation of "Nicholas the Saintly" as one of their hymns attests. I knew that the title Santa Claus came from the Dutch ***Sinterklass***. But before I saw his icon, heard the stories of his life, and realized that the person depicted most often in a sleigh, drawn by reindeer, was also a saint, things started to move in me. And since Nicholas was a bishop, then most likely first he was a presbyter. He celebrated the Eucharist, for Heaven's sake! (Literally…for people's sake and Heaven's destination…)

In my ignorance, there was an awareness that some families in America would put their shoes outside their door and expect something from St. Nicholas on his feast day. To me, that seemed like an appetizer to the coming Christmas gift-feast. I remember feeling sorry for the kids around the world who only celebrated that and missed out on the fun of department store lines to sit on a pudgy man's lap and were deprived of the chance to learn catchy songs that warned us to "watch out" because someone was coming to town. On the other hand, these children might have had fewer nightmares or significantly less fear of the dark in December.

If anyone had ever asked me as a child who Nicholas of Myra was, I would not have had a single clue. Wasn't Myra the character Penny Marshall played on the *Odd Couple* TV sitcom in the 1970's? (No, that's Myrna. Too much television is akin to too many Santa Clauses…) Myra, I've learned, is where Nicholas died on the sixth of December in 343 in modern-day Turkey, a place where no flying reindeer are ever spotted. The tomb of Nicholas actually oozes holy oil that is believed to have healing power. Take that, Rudolph and friends! I dare anyone to make a cartoon Christmas special and draw millions of viewers to the true, mystical version of St. Nicholas. It seems that they would struggle getting sponsors, with the exception of Wesson Cooking Oil. (Can you hear the ad man pitching a commercial: "Oil Be Home for Nicholas?!?")

In parishes where I have served, the "real" Nicholas gets his mention in religious education classes, in Catholic schools, but often the holiday décor and songs the children sing are virtually the same as public schools, except for the nativity scenes. So I have developed a passion to teach that "santa" means holy, means saintly. Godly! But it hasn't been easy. Parents of small children are understandably nostalgic and emotionally fused to the red-suited person who comes down the chimney with gifts in pop culture lore.

One parish had a religious education director who agreed instead of the annual Breakfast with Santa to hold a Breakfast with St. Nick. We had a gentleman dress up as the bishop/saint in Byzantine vestments and a crown. Yes, he posed for pictures and handed out candy canes. But it was a very tough sell. One little child went up to Art Caruana, the volunteer in Nicholas' bishop garb, and said: "We're going to the mall later to see the REAL Santa!" Kids say the darndest things, but haven't we painted ourselves into a dark corner where pop culture and faith need to meet and converse, but many have refused to open the invitation?

I wrote *Holy Good St. Nicholas* in an attempt to bridge the make-believe aspects of Mr. Santa with the real person. For Nicholas-lovers, the God-center of Advent and Christmas clearly offers a tangible way to tie in holiness and gift-giving in order for virtue to take the place of fairy-tale and make-believe. That said, the church's treasure trove of saint stories does include a kind of fiction-flavored narrative called hagiography. From the Greek, it uses a kind of story-telling not necessarily to be literally/historical fact, but rather illustrate, magnify, and even exaggerate the glorious virtues of a canonized saint.

My second St. Nicholas song, *We Three Kids*, includes some of those tales.

Here's verse 1, (sung to the familiar tune of *We Three Kings*):

We three sisters, filled up with fright
Ladies, yes, but not "of the night"
Sin will hurt you, we want virtue
Help us Lord, in our plight.
Oh, oh... Prayers are all that we can say
Nicholas, come save the day
More than kind-did-he
Give with charity
Holy Saint, won't you stay?

The most well-known is the story of three daughters of a poor man who needed money for dowries. Their poverty was so great that, as the story goes, the daughters might end up sold into slavery. St. Nicholas reportedly put some coins in a sack, and tossed them in an open window. (But, as he discovered the best attempts of anonymous donors often find their identity revealed!) A more dramatic version of the story says that the young ladies may have had to partake in the world's oldest profession (and I don't mean carpentry!!) so that their family could survive. Nicholas' generosity saves them not only from financial destitution but a life of prostitution; therefore, our saint saved them not only from bodily death but the spiritual death of mortal sin.

Have you ever heard that St. Nicholas is also the patron of pawnbrokers? The three donations for the daughters mentioned in verse one of my song have sometimes been symbolized not in a sack of gold coins but as golden orbs. The three-ball symbol of the pawn shop is actually tied into that tradition. And the practice of shoes left by the fireplace as well as stockings hung by a chimney are Nicholas-related, for some choose to include the details that the monetary gift landed in the girls' shoes that were drying out by the fire. Or that their wet winter stockings were drying. Either way, St. Nick deserves credit for these practices.

Verse 2 has another very amazing story:

We three sons were caught in a jam
Bathed in brine as salty as ham
When they pickled us, God sent St. Nicholas
Now we're his biggest fans...
Oh, oh... Saint of Myra, can you see
"Nick at Night" has set us free
Now we're living
Through his giving
3 happy lads are we!

I had not heard the story of the three young men until I met Fr. Bertha. It's another one you might not use as a bedtime story for pre-school children unless you want to be awakened for nightmare-erasing duty at 2:00 AM.

Three young lads are said to have been theology students on their way to Athens. A wicked innkeeper robbed and murdered them, and their bodies were hidden in a vat of brine. St. Nicholas miraculously came and stayed at the same inn. During the night, in a dream the Lord showed him the killing, so Nicholas awoke, found them, and prayed, and they came back to life! This wonder-working can inspire seminarians not to get pickled and I can use it in meditation to heal my strong aversion to pickles. Isn't hagiography fun?

The third verse of *We Three Kids* is my own reflection and attempt to tie together Christian faith and the gifts that Jesus gives to our lives as disciples. It can also serve as a clarifying nod to our non-Catholic friends who might mistakenly think that we worship saints. We don't and never have, so one phrase says we "hope to honor Nicholas best…" and "may it please us to know Jesus…" The final line points to Heaven as any good, saintly life will do for us.

We are children, gifted and blessed
Hope to honor Nicholas best
Pray for others, sisters, brothers
God takes you through each test

Oh, Oh…make us icons as we go
Prayers for peace, God's love we'll show
May it please us to know Jesus
Heaven's gifts He'll bestow!!

There's a fantastic website that promotes the real historical person St. Nicholas of Myra. On that site (www.stnicholascenter.org) you can find countless resources for connecting the popular notions of Santa Claus to the human being whose sanctity can inspire our lives beyond December 6th or 25th for that matter. There are coloring pages, as well as images of icons of St. Nicholas. Remember, the Orthodox and Eastern churches are really the leaders in teaching about this great saint. We Romans and other Christians could eventually catch up with them, but at this point I'd say we've barely ***nicked*** the surface!

There's even a page on the website where you can hear songs. My *Holy, Good St. Nicholas* is there, so give it a listen!

WE THREE KIDS
(Tune: "We Three Kings" New Lyrics by Fr. Bill Quinlivan)

We three sisters, filled up with fright
Ladies, yes; but not "of the night"
Sin will hurt you, we want virtue
Help us, Lord, in our plight…

Oh—oh…Prayers are all that we can say
St. Nicholas, come save the day
More than kind-did-he give with charity
Nicholas, won't you stay?

V. 2 We three sons were caught in a jam
Bathed in brine as salty as ham
When they pickled us, God sent Nicholas
Now we're his biggest fans...

Oh—oh… Saint of Myra can you see
"Nick at night" has set us free
Now we're living—through his giving
Three happy lads are we!!!

V. 3 We are children, gifted and blessed
Hope to honor Nicholas best
Pray for others, sisters, brothers
God takes you through each test

Oh—oh…Make us icons as we go
Prayers for peace, God's love we show
May it please us to know Jesus
Heaven's gifts He'll bestow!

II. PRAYERS FOR THE ADVENT SEASON

A Prayer for an Advent Heart

O Lord of all life, who put creation into motion and manifested your presence from eternity into time, we seek your graces and gifts for a holy season of Advent. In our world, we often find ourselves caught in a rush; we yearn for the future and sometimes hurry through the present. In the gift of the present moment, your presence makes our hearts into treasuries of Advent waiting. O Christ, who came, Christ who is returning, may your being our Emmanuel teach us to savor and live fully where we are now: on a journey of faith. Give us Advent hearts, so that instead of being pre-occupied with Christmas presents, we will quietly, prayerfully embrace the now, this moment, this day as a gift from you. We ask this in the Holy Name and presence of Jesus Christ, Our Lord. Amen.

Prayer before Beginning a Christmas Shopping List

Come, Holy Spirit, whose creative flow of gifts are needed for a truly holy Advent season. Before the blank page, I pray, asking your wisdom in my creative planning and selection of gifts to give this Christmas. Lord, bless me with joy so that this process may not become burdensome or anxious. Pour out your grace, which means *gift*, that I might discern thoughtful choices that both express my love and echo yours. O Spirit of prudence, guide my decisions regarding my financial ability to be generous. May each idea for making or buying a gift be accompanied by prayer that I may always grow in virtue. Inspire me, so that the ideas for presents be practical enough to be useful, yet clever enough to surprise. And Lord of providence, may my Christmas giving include not only those friends and loved ones to whom I plan to give, but also the poor and needy who are not as blessed as I. Spirit of Love, anoint my list-making, shopping, and sharing. In the name of Jesus, the gift of the Father, I pray. Amen.

A Gift-Wrapping Prayer

Lord of Advent joy and the mystery of the Incarnation, my prayer before wrapping these gifts is to veil them in mystery for eventual revelation, just as Christ was wrapped in human flesh and His perfect love revealed our salvation! I praise you, Lord, for the resources that allowed for their purchase, and I anticipate the giving of gifts as a living echo of the Epiphany. The Magi laid gifts before you in your infancy, not knowing that your body, your own Sacred Heart would be pierced for the world's salvation.

Your gift of Baptism has clothed us all in Christ, so that His life story might continue to be told through his mystical Body, the Church. As the decorative paper and bows add to the festivity of the coming feast, may we who give to each other acknowledge the wondrous feast of our Savior's birth, the perfect gift of Bethlehem, Christ Jesus Our Lord! Amen.

A Christmas Baker's Prayer

Sweet Jesus, as we arrange the ingredients and implements for baking Christmas treats, we pause to intentionally invite you into this kitchen! Perhaps in the home at Nazareth you watched Our Lady in her baking and food preparation. We welcome you to this humble home and thank you for the recipe of a holy life, that we strive to follow in our preparation for Christmas. Appreciative of the time to dedicate to this labor of love, and mindful of those who will enjoy them, we pray as we work.

As the various parts of a recipe are mixed, may we rejoice that Heaven and Earth, Divinity and humanity have been wondrously blended together in you, God's Son whose birth we celebrate soon. While rolling out the dough, we recall your humility as well as the simple, lowly shepherds of Bethlehem. In choosing various cookie-cutters, we marvel at the variety in your creation while respecting each person's individuality.

And when we frost, decorate, or slice the baked goods, may we see these treats as signs pointing us to the Bread of Life, the Holy Eucharist, the holiest food on earth! May we live this Advent as a time for our spiritual life to rise in the yeast of your grace. Please bless the work of our hands and all the ways we prepare for the sweetest shared meal of Christmas Mass. We pray through Christ, Our Lord. Amen!

A Christmas Decorator's Litany

(while assembling a Nativity scene/creche)

1. **O CHRIST, AS CHRISTMAS NEARS…**

-may we assemble the manger with prayerful hearts…
-may we be reminded by these sheep that we are your flock…
-may these shepherds remind us to pray for priests, deacons and bishops…
-may devotion to Our Lady grow this Advent with our every "Yes"…
-may St. Joseph's example of humility and holy silence inspire our days…
-may the Bethlehem star point us always to Heaven's glories…

REFRAIN: **AT THE WONDER OF YOUR BIRTH**

(while hanging ornaments and garlands)

2. O JESUS, WHO PARTICIPATED IN SACRED FESTIVALS...

-help us recall that human life is as fragile as the ornaments we hang...
-help us find ways to work for Christian unity as we string the garland...
-help us see the Church as the center of our lives as we assemble Christmas villages...
-help us discover new ways to enter deeply into feasts and holy days...
-help us to cherish our sacred spaces and participate joyfully in the liturgy...

REFRAIN: **WITH THE ABIDING GIFT OF FAITH.**

(while stringing lights, decorating fireplaces, placing candles)

3. O LORD OUR GLORY AND LIFE...

-shine your light through us to the world that more people may come to know you.
-shine radiant mercies on all who see the lights we hang to make this home festive.
-shine a warming glow through our fireplace as a reminder of your heart's burning divine love
-shine hope and healing through every Christmas candle, and draw us to yourself.

REFRAIN: **IN A WORLD THAT NEEDS YOUR LIGHT!**

Prayer In Preparation For An Advent Penance Service

Lord, send your Spirit of Truth into my mind, heart, and soul as I prepare myself to receive the Sacrament of your Mercy. In this season of holy longing, grant me a deep desire to name the darkness that has found its way into my life. Open me to what the Advent scriptures reveal, that I am among the "people in darkness" who have "seen a great light."

Like the dusk hours of early winter, I have let shades of pride, selfishness, and all that flows from those sins settle into my attitudes and distort my perceptions. But, like the candles on the Advent wreath's purple hues, a spark of your saving light can ignite a repentant heart and make reconciliation a reality.

As my honest admission of sinful choices leads to a contrite, sorrowful confession, may the blush of shame on my face, like the rose candle on the wreath, be transformed in your grace. As Gaudete joy exults in the nearness of Christ's birth, may my face be changed to reflect sweet joy as I seek your mercy through a sincere Advent sacramental reconciliation.

Finally, Lord, I pray for the priest-confessor who will be your instrument of healing mercy. May Christ the Good Shepherd inspire him to lovingly guide this once-lost sheep back to you, and direct my soul toward Christmas peace!! Amen!

A Prayer Before Writing/Signing Christmas Cards

My Lord, I ask you to bless the time I will now spend writing and signing these greeting cards. Stir up your Spirit in me so that my words may blend with the artist's design to bring tidings of comfort and joy.

Give me an un-hurried, evangelizing sense of purpose, that beyond a "Merry Christmas and Happy New Year" there be words that express love, hope and appreciation. Let the message of Christ's birth be centered in my thinking as a desire to make these cards short epistles and greetings in the Lord's awesome mystery across town, across the world, or across the street.

As I address envelopes, may I be as diligent as the census-takers of Bethlehem on the night of Christ's holy birth. May the list of names be a reminder to include all the families in my prayers throughout Advent, Christmas, and the coming year. Sensitize me, Lord, to remember which friends and family have suffered the loss of a loved one since last Christmas, and which people have been undergoing treatment for serious illness.

Let the joy of Christ guide my words as I share the happiness of the couples who will celebrate their first Christmas with a new baby or the return of college students on semester breaks.

Fill my heart with gratitude for the people you have placed in my life and my family's as I seal the envelopes and attach postage. For we are all recipients of the gift of Jesus from the Father, who "cared enough to send us the very best…" Bless these cards and all who will deliver them and every person who reads them through Christ our Lord. Amen!

Children's Prayers For Advent/Christmas

(7 prayers could perhaps be one each day, repeated for the 4 weeks of Advent)

1. Lord Jesus, this Advent, let me listen to the caring shepherds that you have given me: my parents, older siblings, teachers, coaches, and neighbors. As you were once a child who learned obedience, give me the grace to do the same!

2. Let me look for silence in this season of expectation. Help me turn down the noise in the world and pray to you help me to listen for your voice in my heart.

3. I ask for your grace to be better at sharing the things I have. As Christmas comes near, the gift of God's only Son is shared by the Heavenly Father. Many children do not have the blessings that I have received, so I wish to become more generous.

4. As I grow in my faith, Jesus, and hear the story of your birth every year, show me how to be more like the angels who sang "Glory to God in the Highest." I want to live your Glory all year, but especially in Advent and Christmas.

5. People often say that this season is for children. Lead me, Lord, to pray often for the children in this world who are without a home, whose families are broken, or who do not have freedom to express their faith without danger. I pray for peace, and want to be a peacemaker always!

6. Lord, when I am shy about singing at school or church, help me try to do it for you. The songs and hymns of Advent and Christmas are loved by so many, and I want to add my voice! May my Guardian Angel to sing with me, so that my life becomes a song.

7. With Advent prayers and the coming of Christmas, help me, Jesus, not to think too much about presents, except the gift of your life. When I remember that, may all the other parts of our celebration point me back to you.

   I pray all this as a child of God, in Jesus' Holy Name. Amen!

Prayer For Those Who Are Suffering This Christmas

Heavenly Father, you hold all of creation in your hands. As we prepare for the awesome feast of Christmas, turn our hearts in prayer towards those whose lives are more sorrowful than joyful mysteries at this time.

It was your great compassion and desire to save us that caused you to send your Son, born in Bethlehem. To a suffering world in darkness, in need of a savior, you gave this perfect gift. And we now ask your grace for those most in need of your presence in their lives.

Bless those who suffer chronic pain, the grieving, the refugees, and homeless. Inspire your people to be generous in their outreach to those in prison and their families, to people in hospice care, and to victims of emotional and physical abuse. Send your healing grace to the addicted, that they might find treatment and healing.

Lord, have Mercy on the mentally ill, on couples whose marriages are strained or broken. Help them know that Jesus is our Wonder-Counselor, our Prince of Peace. May those who lack hope and languish in darkness begin to see the great light of Emmanuel, God-with-us!

Remind us, Lord, never to take for granted our blessings of health and well-being. The holly and ivy of our festive season can also symbolize the thorns of Jesus' crown, and the blood He shed for our salvation. In a similar way, the wood and nails of the manger that holds the infant Jesus foreshadow His saving sacrifice on the cross.

We praise You, O Lord, for bearing all our ills and for offering us the promise of a remedy for our suffering when we unite our crosses to yours. Come, Lord Jesus, hear our prayer. Amen.

Advent Prayer for Families

Father of all, let us intercede for our families in this beautiful season of expectation. As Christmas nears, grant us each the grace to see the family's connection to your wondrous plan of salvation. We pray for the older members of our clan, especially, those whose health seems to be a shared concern. Lord, bless them with Advent hope that Christ will be their companion on life's journey. We praise you for the gift of wisdom that their years have offered them and us.

Thank you, O God, for all the children in our lives, and particularly those we will visit this Christmas. Help us to encourage their growth in your grace as we recognize the exuberance of youth. And also, for the young adults and teens, we pray for your Holy Spirit's guidance—and Christmas joy in our gathering.

O Jesus, the coming feast of your Incarnation can teach us all to love one another more fully. May we find a sincere repentance in our Advent confessions to forgive past hurts and misunderstandings among family members. May this coming Christmas be abundantly blessed with peace as your gift—and may that exchange set the tone for all other gift-giving.

Lord, remind us as a family of faith that the birth of our Savior is the first reason we gather. In contrast to the "inns with no room," may our hearts always make room for new additions to our family. And give us an abiding gratitude for having shared past Christmas seasons with our loved ones who have departed.

May this Christmas be filled with surprises and delights, as well as the familiar comfort and joy of our church and family traditions. We ask this through Christ Our Arriving King. Amen.

A Christmas Caroling Prayer

(Each song title could be sung…by all, or designated soloists)

O COME ALL YE FAITHFUL and sing like the ***ANGELS WE HAVE HEARD ON HIGH*** of God's ***JOY TO THE WORLD***, our ***SWEET LITTLE JESUS BOY***! Hey--***DO YOU HEAR WHAT I HEAR***? If so, ***GO, TELL IT ON THE MOUNTAIN***, for from ***THE FIRST NOEL***, and ***IN THE BLEAK MIDWINTER***, that there came an ***O, HOLY NIGHT***. Lord, bless us, for ***HERE WE COME A WASSAILING*** about the ***LITTLE TOWN OF BETHLEHEM***. May each of our carolers who break this ***SILENT NIGHT*** with song come closer to the one born ***AWAY IN A MANGER***. And to those listening who ask "***WHAT CHILD IS THIS?***" may we witness like ***GOOD KING WENCESLAUS, ON THE FEAST OF STEPHEN***"… So we walk the streets of our neighborhood, where people ***DECK THE HALLS WITH BOUGHS OF HOLLY***, while ***WALKING IN A WINTER WONDERLAND*** that all might know that ***CHRIST THE SAVIOR IS BORN, CHRIST THE SAVIOR IS BORN. AMEN!***

Advent Prayer For Eucharistic Adoration

Lord Jesus, we praise you in your real and enduring presence in the Most Blessed Sacrament!

This time of adoration during Advent is a precious gift. While we have come to give you worship, to commit our time and fix our eyes on you, let us be awed. You are the same Christ whose birth caused Heaven's angels to sing "Glory to God in the highest."

In our silence, an Advent symphony rises in our hearts. Long before the first words of *O, Come All Ye Faithful* are sung at Christmas Mass, we respond to its beloved and familiar refrain: "O come, let us adore Him, Christ the Lord!"

To be with you is our privilege, so we acknowledge your countless graces in our lives. O Jesus, we also lay all of the gifts we have received in our lives here at your feet. Lord, you are the fulfillment of human longing for communion with God. Our family of faith, as we gather on the Sundays of Advent, seeks to renew devotion to you. While our calendars in Advent can over-flow with social engagements which include music and festivity, this time we spend together fills us with gratitude, hope, and healing. Treasured time in your presence touches the souls in unique ways.

In sacred silence, hymns of praise rise up to you from our hearts not needing words. As we kneel, bow, or prostrate ourselves or sit in your Holy Presence, fill us with wonder at your Eucharistic Mystery. Like the shepherds and Magi of Bethlehem in Sacred Scripture, we come before you. Advent allows us to pray with Our Lady, your Mother, and St. Joseph as adopted members of your Holy Family.

To be with you… simply acknowledging your Lordship, savoring your presence…in prayerful peace… O come….let us….adore Him… Christ the Lord!!

Advent Mysteries of the Rosary

1. **The Expectation of Israel**
   For generations, O Lord, your chosen people awaited the coming Messiah. Immersing themselves in your Law and the Prophets, through the history of Israel you made them chosen people of the promise. The words of Isaiah, which we hear in our Advent liturgies were repeated, learned, and prayed.... *The people in darkness have seen a great light*... Our Lady and St. Joseph lived that sacred faith tradition as part of the pilgrim people. We wait through each Advent, seek inner light, and trust in your promises that lead us closer to Christ, our light, the fulfillment in every age.

2. **The Ponderings of Mary's Heart**
   As children of the Immaculate One, our hearts reflect on her life of prayer and seek your will, Lord. In significant moments, she "*kept all these things, pondering them in her heart*." Her human heart was troubled as it pondered. So we meditate on the time between the Annunciation and her "*fiat--let it be done*." We don't know the length of time it took, but the Archangel Gabriel waited in serenity. This would be the first of many pondering points in the Blessed Virgin's life, as she sets a beautiful example for us to prayerfully reflect in Advent. May your will, Lord, be our most precious hope. And may the heart of the Mother of God envelop our hearts when we find

ourselves wondering, wandering, and seeking Christ's Peace, awaiting His second coming as well as the feast of His first coming at Christmas.

3. **The Discernment of St. Joseph**
   In harmony with the Blessed Mother's pondering was the discernment of St. Joseph. This "*upright and just man,*" a faithful Israelite in the line of David had free will like ourselves. After his betrothal to Mary, news of her pregnancy caught him by surprise. Soon, a dream informed his decision. But between those two events he would struggle and pray with no easy or immediate answer. St. Joseph's ability to discern well testifies to his faith and trust in God. Our lives often present situations that are not easily resolved. May St. Joseph intercede for us as we reflect on his witness.

4. **The Call and Journey to Bethlehem**
   Sacred Scripture tells us of the census called by Caesar, and the Holy Family's participation in that event. In the context of our faith, can we not see God's hand at work and their call to go to the simple place where the Lord desired His Son to be born? As Christmas nears many people prepare for travel, so Advent offers a poignant time to assess the level of discipleship within each our hearts. St. Joseph and Our Lady took a journey over hills and across rough terrain to participate in the census. We, also are called to be counted as their family through the holy child born at Bethlehem. May we experience the call and deeply spiritual journey through time with discipleship as our passport to prayerful days anticipating Christmas.

5. **The Search for a Birthplace**
   When Mary's time had come to give birth, a new dilemma arose: no room in Bethlehem's inns. The fulfillment of the ancient promise of a child, born to save, was very near. The Lord's providence would lead them to a simple stable, but until that was found, the impending birth brought a new test for their trust in God. In our lives, we must determine the church in which we'll celebrate Christ's birth. We decorate homes and churches with a crèche remembering that holy birthplace. But our souls still long for the eternal home toward which only Christ's grace can guide us—a place prepared for us in the Kingdom of Heaven. The search for a place for Christ to be born is recalled today especially when we hear of refugees and migrants. Our hearts' call to ongoing conversion includes both a sense of being "on the way" as well as "not there yet."

   Lord, guide our longings and search for you this coming Christmas!

III. CHRISTMAS CHAPTERS

Come To Christ This Christmas

As the sun is setting Christmas Eve
When the wreath of Advent takes its leave
Stores and shops and malls all start to close
It's time to do just what we planned and chose
But first, why not-

Come to Christ this Christmas
Find a church and go.
Life without Him misses
The reason why God was humbled low
Bring a friend and worship, on this special day
Come alive this Christmas.
Hear the Word, sing a hymn and pray!

Some come first to claim a favorite pew
But best believers will make some room for you.
Chances are, the music you will know
Familiar, well-loved melodies can show
We all need to-

Come to Christ this Christmas…

Some years we're preoccupied, distracted
Hurrying to wrap a gift, you cracked it!
The perfect one is lying in a manger
His mission-- a world and whole-life-changer
As you are…why not just—

Come to Christ this Christmas!

"I get so anxious when Christmas shopping," people say. We've all had experiences that "I don't know her size…and I am *NOT asking…*" moment. My theory is that this situation brought about the birth of the gift certificate and gift card! What do you buy for the person who "has everything"? Desperately, often while wandering around a mall or store, we try to force the process: "Okay-what does the person who has everything need more than one of??"

These are logical and common questions. Isn't the answer always that a gift can almost never completely express our care? That is, unless we give something of ourselves. Money talks so they tell us. Yes, in some social circles it screams at the other end of the spectrum; it barely whispers. But for the average person (and I consider myself happily average!) money sort of speaks quietly almost hoarse; like a finalist in a Christmas caroling marathon. The voice can squeak or not let out every intended sound, so *Joy to the World* becomes *Oy to the World*. (On a side note, that was a phrase used on Fran Drescher's TV show *The Nanny*. The animated/cartoon Christmas episode was an instant classic, to my taste!)

RUN TO CHRIST AT CHRISTMAS

Christmas 1988 was a pivotal, game-changing one for my immediate family- Dad had died that January. We had all mourned his loss in our own ways. The prior Christmas was very difficult, to say the least, since he had been in the Veteran's Hospital since October after the removal of a brain tumor and radiation therapy. On Christmas day 1987, or late Christmas Eve, he either suffered a stroke or the re-growth of the tumor had suddenly left him non-responsive. I have clear memories of driving up Bailey Avenue in Buffalo to visit, seeing the streets and store fronts decorated for the season. Normally that would excite that Christmas-loving child in me, but in those dark days even Amy Grant Christmas cassettes in the car were not working their usual magic.

Our preparation for celebrating Christ's birth can often take our attention off in distracting detours. But life (and death) has a way of calling us back to basics. Jesus came to us born in Bethlehem. And discipleship begins over and over when we come to Him. We turn to the Lord in our most broken state in our misery and sorrow. In God's amazing ways, it seems that He considers that a precious gift even when we might feel as if we're far from bringing our "best self."

Christmas 1987 was tense and stressful in my family with Dad's medical condition on our minds. But as we often discover, the pain was mixed with joy. My nieces and nephews were very young, a mix of toddlers and infants. There's always that instinct to make Christmas merry for the little ones. And their very presence becomes a living reminder of life's cycle as new life begins and other lives come closer to their end.

1988 was winding down toward the late fall "holiday season" and the family consensus was to change our Christmas traditions. Something new and different, we hoped, would lessen the sense of dread and loss as our first Christmas without Dad approached.

PICK A CATEGORY

My sister Mary was working at a not-for-profit organization which helped coordinate an Adopt-A-Family program. At Thanksgiving we committed to sponsor a less fortunate family so that we could focus outside ourselves. The plan worked very well, and at the same time we decided that for a simplified gift exchange in our time of grief, Christmas shopping seemed more difficult. Between the main course of Thanksgiving and the pies, we came up quickly with three gift categories. Each person would select one name from a hat, and then our intention was to be silly and/or creative in selecting things under the agreed upon themes. Examples: something green, something edible, and something you'd wear on your head. The total spent on all three should not exceed $25. This allowed us to be more generous to the adopted family.

Being Irish and a wee bit competitive in the area of creative thinking, the gifts chosen were mostly silly. Something green could be a can of toy slime or a dollar cleverly wrapped. The emergence of the everything-for-a-dollar stores couldn't have been more perfectly timed. A thrifty person could find gifts in all three categories for as little as $3.00.

Category Christmas immediately became our family's preferred way of handling the gift routine. It flourished for about fifteen years. As time wore on, we eventually went through just about every color in the rainbow, including one year, "something plaid" when I got a roll of Scotch tape with the accompanying explanation that there was plaid on the packaging! I must admit that the majority of the in-laws were never as enthusiastic as my siblings and I were. But we outnumbered them by factoring in the single family members.

Probably the peak of challenge and creativity was the category "something dusty from Dunne's." There was a neighborhood drug store (where my brother Pat once worked during college) across the street from our church. In the decades of its history, there was a tendency for the merchandise on the back shelves (or lower ones) to accumulate dust. The trick with this category was that you had to find something with dust on it and ***leave it intact***! Nobody had a problem locating a dust-covered item, and we laughed ourselves silly as one person received a large mouse trap, coated in dust and others were given various personal care products in boxes or plastic bottles so dusty that the FBI could use them to track finger-prints. One person even put his dusty item into a plastic zip-locked storage bag to preserve the particles of…history.

A Song's Incarnation

From your heavenly throne to a virgin's womb
From a God who saves to the inn with no room
World in silence can't hear the heavens' ovation
You came, Love's Incarnation. Jesus-- Love's Incarnation!

One reason why Christmas seems to have such universal appeal might be the permanent link between Love and the Incarnation. Even those who struggle to find joy as Christmas approaches might be able to hang on to a basic agreement: Christmas and Love are united in a way that never can be separated. Those gifted with faith can go farther: divinity and humanity are bound in a perfect love in Jesus the Word made flesh.

The chilly, rainy morning on which I write this chapter happens to be my parents' wedding anniversary. Sixty-three years ago on May 2, 1953 they took their love to the altar of St. Teresa of Avila Church in South Buffalo. And in the sanctuary, in the presence of Love Incarnate, they exchanged vows and rings. It's all part of the same magnificent plan of salvation!

The evangelist John begins his Gospel with words that include "And the word was made flesh and dwelt among us." (John 1:14) That word-made-flesh concept is what we theologically describe as the Incarnation. Also, what strikes me as I write this on my parents' wedding anniversary is that the Catholic church celebrates the feast of St. Athanasius today.

Now that name might not bring to mind ten friends who were named after him. That has to truly humble some saints, but Athanasius is a Doctor of the Church and he literally suffered through exiles for standing up to the heresy of Arianism. So our oversight has to seem a minor offense. The heretic Arius taught that Christ was not really the Son of God: In other words, one can say this in a figurative sense, but not in a literal sense. Because this would mean that there was no actual Incarnation. To the Catholic tradition this was very much an error.

So, friends of Advent and Christmas, we owe St. Athanasius a debt of gratitude. Because he sacrificed much to make clear that love was incarnate in Christ, the Word was made flesh. Without this dogma, the word is spoken but not made tangible. It would be as if Jim and Kass Quinlivan said "I love you" on May 2nd 1953 but never let it be lived through their bodies becoming one in flesh. And if that never happened, you'd be either reading a blank page now, or re-reading A Christmas Carol in your preparations for Christmas. But if St. Athanasius hadn't defended Christ's incarnation, we'd all be pagans with no single reason to deck the halls or fill the churches. Undoubtedly, some of us would be in synagogues, patiently waiting for Him.

There are cable television networks that produce countless romantic movies from mostly a secular perspective of Christmas. While some people who dive right into that marathon of mush, uh—I mean, sweet film experiences…to me, they lack any overt faith focus making them as substantial as red and green cotton candy. Fluffy and sweet, but no meat! After all, the word incarnation has to do with meat/flesh in its highest meaning, and directly refers to Jesus Christ, the Eternal Word, becoming one of us to save us. Albeit remaining –as a mystery – and a divine person the whole time.

In my experience, I'll freely admit that Advent to Christmas has a healthy dose of both the sacred and the secular. But the longer I sing carols and watch repeats of animated reindeer television specials, I find that the entertainment doesn't segue naturally into Christmas. My years have continued to move the spotlight to the manger, the baby born in Bethlehem, and the awesome mystery that draws us to Christ. It's not that I haven't tasted and enjoyed the Christmas cotton candy as an appetizer of the season. I can probably apply some religious meaning or moral out of a favorite song of the season that never mentions Jesus by name. Mostly because if it's about love, He is that love… incarnate.

From a census called to old Bethlehem town
From a hope near-lost to a simple stable found
No mere words can describe that God-is-near-sensation
Love's Incarnation, Jesus-- Love's Incarnation!

The verses of my song, *Love's Incarnation*, attempt to do what I'd hope most Christian preachers address from the pulpit when surrounded by Advent wreaths for four weeks, as the season progresses and the environment moves closer to the feast where we celebrate Christ's birth. A pet peeve that we who have experienced theological education share is that it seems a trite understatement to call Christmas Jesus' "birthday." Except that, for young children, it has become a very highly-relatable term, it is also better to express it more as a description of mystery.

There is not a lot of debate needed as to whether Jesus Christ was born exactly on December 25th. In fact, the Orthodox Christians don't use that day, but do use something closer to Epiphany. Most important then is pinpointing *whom* and *what* we celebrate rather than being historically attached to a calendar date. So the mostly tightly-wound among us may relax, if you think that they have to mail a card to the Son of God by the twenty-fifth of December.

I heard a story once about a well-meaning but confused Catholic catechist who was trying to introduce some small children to the feast of the Immaculate Conception. Long before many dioceses insisted on elaborate training for volunteer religious education teachers, this person was speaking off-the-cuff. Thereby, legend has it, said: "So, kids, what's also miraculous about the birth of Jesus is that Mary said 'Yes' to the Angel Gabriel on the eighth of December and she gave birth to Our Lord on the 25th. Such a short pregnancy! Nothing is impossible with God!"

From the prophets' call, to God's people His delight
From the angels' song to the shepherds in the night
All are gifts from God's hand, our cause for jubilation
Came through Love's Incarnation, Jesus- Love's Incarnation!

GOD'S "TO/FROM" TAG

The initial moment of sparked idea for my song *Love's Incarnation* actually started with the notion of the Heavenly Father's gift of His only-begotten Son not having one of those "to/from" tags we use to label Christmas gifts. They're very helpful for people like me, who after wrapping a few gifts, I can very quickly forget what's under the wrapping paper. So, while it adds an element of surprise when I watch people open the gifts I give, it doesn't help to wrap too early in Advent. Gift exchanges in a group of co-workers, friends, or family, have an un-written rule of equal-gifting. So the last-minute panic of "Is this gift *enough*??" can set in, especially when I wrapped it too far in advance of the gift exchange and I've forgotten what's inside. And when I decided to attach "To/From" tags later. I end up sheepishly saying as they tear off the gift-wrap. "Hmmm… I cannot recall what I got you. So *both of us* are about to be surprised!"

"To/From" tags also help when families share the same design of wrapping paper! But God's gift of our Savior was obviously not explicitly needing a "From" When the Word was made flesh, His whole life would reveal the Father from whom He was sent. And then, after His Paschal sacrifice, Resurrection, and Ascension, we would be invited to go "to" the place of His "from!"

The wonderful, eternal gift of God in Jesus had (and has) the "Heaven to Earth and back to Heaven" story arc. But the narrative of Christ's whole life also takes us step by step from the *fiat* of the Virgin Mary through His ascension and to this moment as we live in His grace. It concludes with God fulfilling every promise of the Kingdom at the final judgment when Jesus returns in glory.

Actually, the better way to look at faith and reflection on divine *Love's Incarnation* happens to be a simple reversal: rather than a "To/From" it's actually a "From/To" I'm just now remembering that I purposely wrote each verse of my song to start with "From:" and then move toward us in- "To:" each consecutive step. Then, to complete the journey, I did shift in the third verse to emphasize that the coming Son of God would ask us to DO something with His gifts. And our lives then offer them back to the giver when we let love become incarnate in ourselves.

To *un-wrap this gift* ***from*** *our God's eternal plan*
To *remain here present,* ***from*** *our falls He helps us stand*
Takes God's Mercy to bring
Our hate and sins' cessation
Love's incarnation, Jesus— Love's Incarnation

Give Me Christmas

There are some who long for sunny shores
Juicy summer peach, savored at the beach
Then there's those who dream of a cruise with Mickey
Or a slot machine within reach.
It might be bizarre—I'm not where you are
There's just one thing for which I pine--
It's the time and season with a Jesus reason
Always singing through my mind

GIVE ME CHRISTMAS, full of joy as new snow falls
GIVE ME CHRISTMAS, sing the carols, deck the halls
From the birth of our Savior 'til the day He comes again
I'll sing "O, Come All Ye Faithful" to
Every who, what, where and when
When you--- **GIVE…..ME……CHRISTMAS!!**

There are days when I find I just
Wanna hear some sleigh bells sing
But I dare not say—it's so far away
Many eye rolls it will bring!
So I bottle up my Christmas dreams
But they'll stay fresh, don't you doubt--
When we reach December 24th you can bet I'm gonna shout…
(GIVE ME CHRISTMAS…)

There is no gift like our Jesus
We'll un-wrap this holy day
Ring the bells up in your steeple
My fav'rite season's on the way-
Someone, PLEASE ***GIVE…ME…CHRISTMAS!!!***

I'll let you in on a little secret. I'm writing this chapter on Half-Christmas! June 25, exactly half a year since the prior celebration, and six months until the next. I posted a message on my Facebook page with a Merry Half-Christmas with an accompanying link to one of my homemade music videos for a song from one of my Christmas CDs. Some may call me half-crazy. And I cannot argue. In fact, any judge or jury of Christmas Sanity also would say that you're half-right. I'll let you decide which half!

Isn't it true that we can spend our lives longing too much for a distant future or a far-away past, and miss the present moment? One twist on that can also be that Advent and Christmas get missed when people have their love of summer too much in mind. I am the first to admit that I have not completely outgrown my Christmas mania from childhood. My preference is to describe myself as having held on to just enough of it to get excited in the off-season. Don't hockey players look forward to tying on their skates in the off-season? I do not think a good hockey referee would accuse me of icing the puck or crossing the blue line. (I cross the red and green line anyway!)

What would we wish for in the off-season for Advent and Christmas? Parishes, schools, and many other organizations need to plan a year of their calendar events in advance. Families the size of ours needed coordination of times, especially with eight people and only one full rest room in the home.

HOW MANY HOLIDAYS?

If genies with wishes were to visit me, unlike beauty pageant contestants who seem to answer "world peace" to just about any question, I would use one wish to do a lifetime Christmas review. *Of course*, I pray for world peace, and if the genie would give me three wishes it sure makes sense to request that one first. I tend to be the reality-spoiler in those fictional situations and suggest that the first wish be for a million more wishes. It would decrease the stress on the decision-maker, wouldn't it?

So-if I could do a Coast Through Christmas Past (Ghosts? No thank you Mr. Dickens. Let me ***coast***...) I would want to go back to my childhood Christmases and observe my parents more closely. When a kid opens a Mr. Potato Head or Tip-It game, especially under the guise that a North Pole visitor left it for him/her, they don't notice a lot of details. Certainly I didn't.

If my theory that Heaven has a divine type of video playback for souls comes true, I would also rewind to see myself again, next to my Dad, helping him decorate the house. If I could watch my family filling a pew at St. Teresa's on Christmas morning, it would be delightful. Our family traditions did not include a vigil Mass on December 24th. Even though the practice of anticipated Masses had barely been introduced, we *always* went to Mass on Christmas morning. Honestly, our beloved parish was hardly cutting-edge in introducing post-Vatican II reforms. We used to joke among ourselves that although Mass was celebrated in English, it still appeared in glorious black and white!

I'd go back to my first choir rehearsal in grade school, when in October we started practicing *Do You Hear What I Hear*. All these years later, I still can see Joe Donohue, my neighbor across the street, who was the organist, at the piano in my old kindergarten room. It would be fun to get a selfie next to young Bill Quinlivan as he realizes that choir practice necessitates the music of Christmas being taught even before Halloween.

Long before there were year-round Christmas stores, we had to wait for the first signs of the season to appear in retail establishments. My friend Fr. Ray Donohue (younger brother of Joe, the organist) and I always shared what some analysts or therapists might call Seasonal Pining Disorder. He's actually surpassed me in that regard in recent decades, but I'll let him write his own book with those details! During our high school years, after Ray got his driver's license, we would drive to pick his mother up from work. So between school dismissal and her time to clock out from her work day, we had a bit of time.

We used to stop at the Southgate Plaza in West Seneca on the way and purposely kept our eyes on the Sears department store in late October. (You can tell how long ago this happened, since so many retail outlets now start selling Christmas decorations and artificial trees even before the leaves change color in fall!) When Sears first began displaying Christmas items, we would be ecstatic. Come to think of it, we didn't even wait until Sears kicked off the season. Every year on the way home from the Erie County Fair, we'd say "Well, now that the fair is over, it's almost Christmas!" and we'd sing Christmas carols in the car all the way home.

I remember many December days in South Buffalo when the last day of school before the Christmas vacation started. My gym teacher would not have recognized me as I ran as fast as a pudgy kid high on vacation anticipation could possibly go. Down Stevenson Street I would hurry, its trees arching over the road and often coated with snow. In my book bag there was a small box of hard candy which the pastor used to give each child as a little gift after the school Christmas assembly. I can see the large, red faux leather chair in front of the gym's stage, and everyone lined up to wish Msgr. Leo J. Toomey a Merry Christmas. In later years, Fr. Basil Ormsby did the gift-giving. Teachers would undoubtedly be almost excited as I as the final bell rang, but they would very carefully instruct us to not have too much of that sugary stuff before we were dismissed. Hey—that had to be why I could suddenly run so fast!

People might think that a Chronic Christmas Enthusiast is the last thing they would want to be. Grumpy Scrooge-like persons have barked. "You can HAVE Christmas!" My life-long sincere response would be... "Thank you. Give me Christmas!"

Evergreen

Evergreen, your name sings hope songs
Ever fresh, purest scent of joy
Your fragrance fills my soul with Christmas
Never lost to this old boy

The deepest woods bow to their maker
The God forever can't define
To celebrate the birth of Jesus
Nothing compares to forest pine!

Evergreen, like faith's supposed to be
I'm out of my tree with great delight
Each fir tree brings Heaven's scent to me
And every Christmas my heart takes flight!

They grow up tall, thin at their peaking
And send their cones cascading down
The only needles lacking greening
Make a blanket for the deer on the ground

Inside our homes, with bright star topping
As light or angels grace their height
Or 'round a wreath, beauty like God's love
Dressed in a coat of snowy white!

Evergreen…like faith's supposed to be

Green has always been my favorite color. In the "age of Aquarius" when people asked what your astrological sign or birth stone were, I ignored talk of Scorpio and topaz. Sorry. My sign is a pine tree; my color is green. Add my Irish heritage to that and you'll understand why when I sing *O Christmas Tree*, it's ***O'Christmas Tree*** with the apostrophe. How my dear, departed friend Msgr. John Zeitler, so proud of his German heritage would really get his *tannenbaum* twisted by that notion! It's okay, no one sees the apostrophe when I sing it. If that offends you, kindly ignore that I said it and read on, okay? **O'Kay??**

My lyric says "*Evergreen, your name sings hope songs*." The color green makes me hopeful. And the site of pine trees growing up a mountainside adds a note of "ever" to the green. The Lord God so often revealed Himself on mountains in the sacred scriptures. While I don't know whether Moses or Abraham had the pleasure of inhaling pine scent atop their respective maker-meeting heights, there's no question in my mind whether Heaven has pine trees. I fully expect that the room prepared for me will have a view of a pine forest.

Our loving God has taught us that He is with us, always and perpetually faithful and present. Evergreens symbolize that strong and consistent truth of our Divine Lord. And in my mind, God wears cologne that smells like pine. How would I know that? Well, truthfully I don't, but that scent is the closest thing to Heaven for my senses. (In the days before Easter, freshly-cleaned church pews that have the sweet smell of Murphy's Oil Soap is a very close second. The silver medal of fragrance Olympics. What wins bronze? Probably chocolate chip cookies.)

Several years ago I wandered into a scented candle store at a mall in summer and began hunting for green pine-scented candles. When I asked a clerk for help, she shared that the vast majority of men who shop for candles at their business ask for pine scent. I was disappointed that they consider that scent a holiday item, and I had to wait until mid-fall to return and stock up. If my memory serves me correctly, I happened to mention my preference for pine-scented candles in a homily once. That December, a supply of gift candles arrived that could have kept the parish church brightly lit in a blackout for three weeks. We priests must be careful what we say about our "likes". It can easily be interpreted as a not-so-subtle hint. To test this theory, I might soon mention while preaching that I love the smell of **full churches.** Let's see if that has the same effect!

When I arrive at a new parish assignment, my eye is instantly drawn to pine trees on the property. While at St. Gregory the Great parish in Williamsville, New York, I enjoyed the sight of two very tall evergreen trees that flanked the church entrance way. My guess of their height would be approximately twenty feet. The number of times I stared at them and wondered how we could decorate them with lights would be many multiples of twenty!

The opportunity finally arrived. As the new millennium and the year 2000 neared and many people were fearing worldwide computer melt-downs, I was proposing to the parish staff that we put lights on those trees. My memory of the financial expense is blurry, but there were some donations that allowed us to put strings of white lights on both trees. Since St. Greg's has been the largest suburban parish in the Diocese of Buffalo for a number of years, it made sense to do something visual to give people a better sense of our size.

At the time there were approximately 5000 families or households in the parish. So my proposal was to put 2500 lights on each tree, so that each one represented a family unit or single household. Most of the staff were supportive of this project, but I recall that the maintenance crew who had to climb the ladder and tend to all the other details had my photo on the dartboard in their break room for some time. By now, years later, the memory of people's faces seeing the lights (and having it explained) has made it worthwhile.

“I *Love* Your Tree!”

Aunt Peg walked into the living room at the height of the Christmas season, stopped and proclaimed “Well!” Then, after a long pause, followed with: “I LOVE your tree!” Margaret Quinlivan Forti was Dad’s only sister. She and my Uncle Joe both worked in education, and she sometimes carried herself like a teacher checking out a student’s project. Her evaluations were decisive, and unlike her brother who raised me, she didn’t hesitate much before she gave a “nay” or “yea.”

If you’ve ever spent considerable time decorating a tree for your home at Christmas, you usually hope and expect that people might comment on it. We were only an artificial tree home for very few years at a time when aging parents insisted that we’d hardly notice the difference. But for the vast majority of years, the Quinlivans have been tree-lot purchasers of freshly-cut pine, sometimes Scotch Pine and in later years the Frasier fir.

The heroically earthy, woodsy types of people will gallantly trudge into a forest to cut their own. They even proudly display the scars from altercations with the wild animals that may have nested under the particular pine they had chosen. In the woods I often wonder if the families of beasts don’t recall the arrival of holiday tree hunters as *The Christmas Chain Saw Massacre*. What happens when these same lumberjack people present a bouquet of flowers to a spouse or date? Do they proudly boast “I picked them *myself*. No florist for me; that’s for wimps!”

If you don't love a fresh pine tree, the whole experience can be very difficult. So, I say love your tree, and be kind to those who persecute you for the way you trim it to fit into your living room. (Political correctness would call that "tree shape shaming"…) Honestly, the shop and purchase day is about the easiest part. You can attempt to haggle with the salesperson, but when it's so cold outside that you cannot feel your feet, nose, or fingers, it's easier to quickly succumb to their lot price. Even if I talk them down five dollars—I then give a tip for the same amount after they hoist and tie it atop my car.

HUG A TREE?

Have you ever noticed that they wrap the trees in plastic mesh straight-jackets? How much less subtle could this symbol be about the questionable sanity that this transaction puts in motion? Yet, we happily restrain our purchase onto the roof of the car and head home. I always get anxious during the seek-and-find part as if they might run out of trees. Along with the annual family negotiation of when it's best to decorate the house, the tree adoption must also be mutually agreeable. Otherwise it's at the mercy of the person paying for this important merchandise.

Fitting the trunk of the tree into a base can be an anxious experience. It reminds me of the story of Cinderella, where every woman in the town tries on her left-behind glass slipper in the hope of marrying the prince. Our family Christmas tree base and several boxes of decorations are what I inherited from my parents' estate. And it was actually all I ever wanted. Because I was Dad's apprentice and ladder-holder for decorating and absolutely obnoxious in my zeal for the season, I was the obvious choice.

Our Christmas tree base is made of cast iron. Doing some research on eBay, I found similar ones described as being manufactured in the 1920s. I knew that Nana Quinlivan had given it to Dad, and the design was quite sturdy. Around the base several painted poinsettias frame light bulb sockets. So this fancy piece of family heirloom, now nearing 100 years old, had the modern convenience of electricity.

After our years of using it at 205 Stevenson, the paint cracked and peeled, and the wires underneath were frayed, which made us a bit *a-frayed* to use it. So I asked a friend, Deacon Dave Velasquez (who's electrically gifted) if he could replace the wiring. He surprised me by also re-painting the poinsettias, and it came out like new, seventy-five years after it was made. It was beautiful! How firm a foundation this cast iron piece of antique art brings to a fir tree, once the bottom of a tree's trunk is chopped and trimmed to a width of about 5.5 inches. Its weight and shape make it virtually tip-proof.

Those who have read my first book (*Made to Praise Him: Finding My Song*) might recall the dramatic story of an un-invited bat in the attic bedroom that I shared with my younger brother, Joe. It was the Christmas tree base with its solid heavy-metal nature that saved us from the bat and sent that flying rodent to meet its maker one summer night.

WE'RE A (REAL CHRISTMAS) TREE-HOUSE!

Once inside, and secured in a base, you ceremoniously free the captive, bound-up bush and let it "breathe" or wait for the branches to open naturally again as it slowly adjusts to a heated home. You can almost hear the furnace giggle and mumble to itself: "Ever *green*, huh? In a few days you'll be calling that thing *Brownie* –ha, ha!" I love that the color green and the evergreen are an image for God's love, always fresh and life-giving. Taking a tree that can endure all seasons (while it has roots, gets water and sun…), and bringing it indoors sure does introduce a whole new definition for hope, right?

The first days of a pine tree's indoor experience allows it to give off its enchanting scent. I'd prefer to think that it's nature's way of blessing the home. But part of me wonders whether it isn't analogous to the sting of a bee or the spray of a skunk in alarm/panic mode and a desperate cry for help… Never mind. I like to think of the first interpretation. I like that better and I'm sticking with it!

These former forest friends oh-so-temporarily share out residences. I know that this relatively brief moment might move some to choose an artificial tree and spray-can fake pine scent. But not me! One must care for this house guest with attentive watering, and listen carefully to every theory of how to keep it fresh longer. Numerous products sold in year-round Christmas stores promise to lengthen the life of a fresh tree. There are also various time-honored and tested recipes for extending post-cut pine lives including aspirin in the water, a shot of vodka, or honey to simulate sap. The results of some of these are negotiable, raising the question of whether the professors of pine had a few too many shots of something else…and that raises the question: who is the *sap* in this scenario?

When its' after-life span comes to an end, a Christmas tree's refusal to drink water and an increase of falling needles bring us to the dreaded removal process. There are large plastic "tree removal" bags that you're supposed to put around the bottom of your tree, to "simplify" their extrication. Simple has ***never*** been my experience of this task. C'mon, people. A thin plastic bag cannot be expected to gently contain dry, pointy, brittle branches. Maybe a large leather wrap, but that would outweigh a dry tree and be exceedingly costly.

The songwriter in me is challenged to write a bit of music to accompany this Porcupine Ballet, our annual attempt to pull it through too-narrow doorways and gracefully escort it to the curb. We're still waiting for the makers of those mesh straight-jackets to come up with a way to re-apply them so as to sail through the doors and around corners. I have a feeling we'd be better off waiting for flying reindeer to land on our roof.

EVERGREENS, EVER-THERE, NEEDLING US LOVINGLY

In negotiations of real vs. artificial tree, fake tree fans argue that they simply *cannot* deal with the fact that Christmas tree needles scatter so well on un-decoration day, and dried-out needles keep showing up months after our curbside pine skeletons are sawdust. They feign horror and disgust while recalling summer days when barefoot family members discovered yet *another* needle left behind in the carpet.

Summer dialogue from a fresh pine tree-loving home:

"You'd like some ice-cold lemonade?

Well, please let me get it for y-OWWWWCH!"

Yes, I've found them, too. No longer green, they are truly more like needles. But my mind will not easily be changed on this issue. In fact, I have come up with another pseudo-scientific theory: the pine needles we step on July 4th may actually inject a small amount of tree-addicting serum into the skin. While admittedly even a fresh pine lover like me might be heard to mutter while running the vacuuming during clean-up or on my knees picking up far-flung needles, "That's it! This was the *last year* for a real tree!!" But there's a year-long cycle that occurs. And Christmas tree addiction gets slowly renewed after the inoculation as Secret Santa Serum works its way to the brain. I've never been much for conspiracy theories. But I'd happily become the national spokesperson for this one!

Post-Christmas blues overcome some. If the labor involved in sending Christmas cards pushes them over the edge, they consider changing to e-mails instead. We may all have talked about it, and some have abandoned certain Christmas traditions. That's their prerogative. But by next year, when barren oaks and maples make the evergreens stand out, by the first week of November when we again find those plastic bags for Christmas tree disposal on store shelves, we think… "Hmmmm…maybe that *would* help catch the needles. I DO LOVE a real tree….."

Sleigh Bells

Sleigh bells, give my heart a Christmas treat
Bright music, makes our caroling complete
I love sleigh bells
Through the year they keep the beat
On my Guardian Angel's feet
I pray bells give you joy for all you're worth
They say bells ring the news of Jesus' birth
So let's play bells with our melodies of mirth
In the season of Joy on the earth!

You can ring out news of His birth, like the angels
God is with us, born as a child
Love has changed all history, incarnate mystery
That the sinners be reconciled!
Sleigh bells...

Kings and shepherds came to see
The only Son of God as He
Laid within the manger asleep
Donkey bells accompanied the Holy Family
No room! But in your heart please keep
Sleigh bells....

When we live His love, we ring out
Like the sleigh bells
Keeping Christ within, through the year
Hope is sprinkled generous as

Snow in December
In His name let faith replace fear!
Sleigh bells...

In the study of psychology and behavior, we were taught that Russian Psychologist Ivan Pavlov's dog was able to associate food to the sound of a bell. Because Pavlov initially noticed that the dog was starting to salivate when the lab assistant who always fed him entered the room (even when he didn't bring food) the canine still made the connection. The research concluded that this kind of reflex was natural, "hard wired" into the dog when the creature mentally associated a certain person with getting dog food. To test and prove that theory, he began to ring a bell when feeding Fido. (Sorry, I didn't get the dog's name. It was perhaps something more Russian, like Vladimir. Because of the subject of this book I say that we should probably just call him Rudolph.) Lots of salivation... experiment worked. Somebody get a mop!

Let me now draw a comparison between Pavlov's dog and me. (No, I will not sit up and beg that you buy this book if you're just flipping through it. But that might not be a bad sales gimmick!) My deeply-planted association has to do with sleigh bells. All I have to do is hear the sound and I feel happy, a joyful and refreshing sense of delight—yes, a treat of sorts!

Why is that? Did my parents load the six children into sleighs for fabulous outdoor winter adventures in farm land near Buffalo? Not at all. Station wagons and church pews were our loading places of choice. So how does a city kid get to love something so clearly used in rural settings? The answer: Firestone Tires! Huh?

Actually, Firestone Christmas albums from the 1960s say it better. Those big orchestra pop singer collections with cover art resembling a wrapped gift. Yes, this gift was given with the purchase of new tires. From what I could find out, the cost was only one dollar for the album. Ah....the good old days!! And we played them and enjoyed the lovely music. Sleigh bells are a sound most often heard on mid-tempo or upbeat Christmas songs, so I wrote my own to try to express my love of the sound. And I felt morally obligated to include them.

Though our Buffalo winters have always had, as Johnny Mathis sings in *Sleigh Ride,* “lovely weather for a sleigh ride together…” I’ve never had a ride in one. It’s okay, I was finally blessed with an authentic set of sleigh bells of my own. So I get to hear the awesome sound and don’t have to deal with horse smells. I’m fine with that.

The first set I found were on a small strap, about six to eight bells. One Advent, I was reading a book by Servant of God Catherine DeHeuck Doherty, foundress of Madonna House in Combermere, Ontario. Her little book, titled *Donkey Bells* made quite an impression on me. It never occurred to me that the beast our Blessed Mother rode upon in the journey to Bethlehem may have worn bells. So verse two of my song mentions donkey bells.

Catherine’s reflections included the concept that Advent is the season of our waiting for the approach of the Holy Family, so we must listen for donkey bells. Once, for my homily on the Fourth Sunday of Advent at St. Luke’s Mission, I decided to strap the small set of sleigh bells onto my right ankle before I processed in. As expected, the little children present were wondering where that sound was coming from. I purposely stamped my right foot in time with the gathering song as I walked. (Once a percussionist, always a percussionist, I guess.) Needless to say, I had to watch my step throughout the liturgy or I would be ringing bells at inappropriate moments.

That Christmas I wrote *Sleigh Bells*. Just like church bells ringing out across the winter sky to summon worshippers for the feast of Christ's incarnation, our witness to His Gospel as part of our preparation for that day has an effect on the world. Even a sound effect, if you strap sleigh bells onto your ankle and you're adventurous enough to wear them during Sunday Mass.

My dear friend Barbara Berger lives in beautiful Elma, New York. She even has a barn, but no horses, reindeer, or donkeys. One of my most prized possessions is a five-foot-long set of full-size sleigh bells she brought up out of her basement one day. Apparently the home's original owner had a team of some sort of beasts of burden. I brought them home and showed them to my housekeeper at the time, Ellen Stilson, a true whiz at cleaning, fixing, and handy-lady work.

"Let me take those home and clean them up for you," she said. The child in me was hesitant for a moment to let go of my new toy, but eventually I gave her the leather strap, and the fifteen or so bells made a lovely sound as she took them to her car. About two days later, Ellen appeared with a set of shiny gold sleigh bells, all signs of dirt and spider webs removed, leather strap polished in a gorgeous dark brown shade. Talk about earning your Christmas bonus!! Those bells have accompanied me on several Christmas recordings as well as virtually every Christmas caroling event of the past fifteen years.

WE ARE THE BELLS

The third verse of the song offers an application that sees our lives like sleigh bells in motion. In a very real sense, the same excitement that my soul feels when I hear my beloved sleigh bells can be experienced by people who encounter a believer in Christ. So it's not so much a sound effect as a faith effect. In the way that the music of these instruments strapped to a horse, pulling a sleigh or plow can be memorable, acts and words of kindness to strangers might also "ring a bell" to them as they recognize Christ within us.

In my area of the world, spontaneous snow-clearing can be a momentous gift. Imagine if we sent out volunteers to clear the snow off every car in a mall parking lot to surprise tired Christmas shoppers. Or you and your family choose an elderly neighbor, widow, or widower, who you know struggles to push a shovel because of arthritic joints. Random acts of snow-plowing, or in some areas sandstorm cleaning could really be a gift that rings out good will.

I recently heard of a practice that one family has that really inspired me. They are a rather large clan, with a number of young adult children and grandkids. Before Christmas, they conspire to surprise a person or family in need, carefully gathering information about what they might donate. Then, at a designated moment, they bring gifts, groceries, and other donations to the door. The doorbell is rung, and they run away as fast as possible so as not to be seen.

In smart-phone photography there's a game called "photo-bombing" where someone stands behind the people posing for a shot and jumps into the picture. This concept might be called Ring and Run, and has to leave the recipients quite shocked and touched by this clever random act of Christmas giving!

BELL-RINGERS

Ringing bells get people's attention. In monasteries, the chimes call the monks and nuns to the chapel for prayer. Many churches have bell towers, yet I've found that a majority of them now have sound systems with pre-recorded bells installed. It creates the illusion that some quasi-bell tolling person or Quasimodo is hiding in the tower pulling a giant rope and causing church bells to ring out across the neighborhood.

Of course, that can also go haywire, because hey-- they're *wired*! I distinctly recall a night when, tucked (by myself) into my bed at Blessed Sacrament rectory in the Town of Tonawanda, I had what I thought was a strange dream that the church bells were ringing. I awoke, though not completely. Chalking it up to a dreams' ability to surprise, I drifted back off to sleep. But an hour later I bolted up in bed as I realized that the bells were ringing. And since we had no Mass scheduled for 2:00 AM, I scrambled for my church keys and hurried over to unplug my electronic employee before angry neighbors might get my phone ringing more than the faux church bells!

Bells ring inside of churches as well as outside. One does not have to climb a steeple to hear them. At Catholic liturgies, a bell signals the beginning of an entrance procession, and altar servers often ring bells during the elevation of the host and chalice as bread and wine become the Body and Blood of Christ. And on special occasions like the Easter Vigil, the first Gloria after six weeks of Lent or the Gloria at Christmas Mass are sometimes also accompanied by bells.

Some churches encourage families with young children to *bring* bells and ring them on cue. A rather creative idea, to involve the kids in a practical/musical way. But I would imagine that instructions must be carefully given. A responsible adult would need to hold said bells in a purse or sealed, locked suitcase until the appropriate moment. I heard that in one church the entrance song and procession were augmented by a cacophony of joyful bells. But then I would imagine it would be a challenge to stop children once they get into the ringing. Come to think of it, doesn't a bell also signal the beginning of a professional wrestling match? Parents as a tag-team versus little Bobby the Bell Boy for the Christmas Mass Championship belt!?

BELL TOWER ROUND

Christ is Born, Christ is Born
Let us adore Him, let us adore Him
Tell the whole world, tell the whole world
Love, Love, Love, Love...

In music I have always loved a counter-point melody or a good descant which is played or sung over the melody to augment and offset it artistically. My friends Mary Beth Harper, Mary Rozak, and Nan Keller do that beautifully on my Christmas CDs. I also have a fascination with the music form called a round. The best known one would be *Row, Row, Row Your Boat*. (One could easily turn that into a fun round: "Snow, snow, on your coat, ice is on the seams. Warily, warily, warily, warily winter's not a dream!"

I have often anchored my songwriting boat in the bay of round-singing. And my *Bell Tower Round* attempts to make the voices ring as if people are bells tolling out simultaneous and slightly different rhythms and notes. Perhaps because my height sometimes makes me appear to tower over others in group photos, I wanted to sing a bell tower song. It's more complicated than *Row, Row, Row*... especially when I'm ambitious enough to try to break a congregation or concert audience into three parts and teach them each a line. Sometimes when I hear myself trying to explain a musical idea, I wonder if I might have *hit my head* on a church bell at some point while climbing into the choir loft.

Christmas Snow

On that holy night, Heaven would bestow
Grace abundant like falling snow
Softly, gently, alight on the people
Sweet salvation to know!
Fragile as a snowflake, soon to heal our heartache
Came as our Redeemer, dawning like the morn
Though our sins be scarlet, for thief and lonely harlot
The Son of purest Virgin Mary has been born!

Many Christmas Eves ago, my whole immediate family was gathering in the house where we grew up. Dad had parked his car in the garage, and I had to get something out of my vehicle, which was parked in the spot next to his. It had snowed steadily most of the late afternoon, and about four of five inches had piled up. In an average winter here in Western New York we call that a normal day. Other areas of the world are thrown into a panic. We're just used to it. Snow kidding!

As I walked up the alley toward the garage, I saw that our blacktopped yard was covered in a smooth blanket of the white stuff. This was at a time long before school classrooms had upgraded from blackboards with chalk to "white boards." But I stopped in my tracks to discover such an untouched, footprint-free blank surface. At that point the moon must have been out, for the fallen snow seemed strangely illuminated.

At first, I decided not to disturb that surface. Instead, I walked around to a side of the yard where Dad's flower beds bloomed in warmer days and carefully stepped into the garage.

After finding what I needed in my car, I had another idea. It suddenly occurred to me that my size 12 boots would be fine writing implements for a snow-covered blackboard. And my heart, enlarged with Christmas joy, needed to express it. (I hadn't yet started writing songs or books. That's how I channel that creative energy now, and it keeps my feet much warmer and drier!)

(Art by Debbie Keenan)

Stepping onto the surface from the hibernating garden, I dragged my boots in a purposeful way until I had written "Merry Christmas" in letters about five feet high. Who would read this? It didn't much matter. Perhaps the next-door neighbors taking a glance out of a second-story window might find in this message a moment of blessing. Or maybe from our dining room's picture window, someone would look out and read it. Would they need to ask who did it? I highly doubt it. But my guess is that the household's "Most Likely to Carol Out of Season" nominee would be the obvious suspect.

Writ large, they say of a life well-lived. Written in boot prints was the message as lasting as the generations since the birth of Christ. Should a low-flying plane give a last-minute Christmas traveler a thrill, I'd be delighted. Even a fly-by Christmas angel doing a nostalgic round-the-globe trek could see the continuing fruits of the first appearance of the choir of angels over a Bethlehem field. Did someone in that holy place drag their sandals around some sand that night and write the same message, in another tongue? I hope so.

Christmas Snow, still brightens up a long night
Jesus comes as Heaven's perfect light
And He stays, that we might learn to love Him
Precipitating grace asks: "Do you get my drift?"

Our backyard on Stevenson Street was our training ground in winter for using the snow blower. (Dad always called it the snow-*thrower*, for some reason.)My mother had indoor winter activities that included plowing through mounds of laundry and a sink forever filled with dirty dishes. Dad had his seasonal challenge to keep our yard, driveway and sidewalk clear. And at a certain age, right around the age where we could take a turn washing dishes…even the good dishes, each of the six of us attended the Jim Quinlivan Snow Removal Academy.

It was so simple. Even a child could do it. So, obviously, six growing children did! As long as the blower's spark plugs were good, there was gasoline in the tank (if someone remembered to drain the gas from the tube that flowed into the engine before temperatures hit the freezing mark) it was a breeze. Actually, it was: prime and pull! A small rubber knob had to be compressed to send gas into the engine, then a rope-chord was yanked to "turn over the engine."

Not one of us (including Dad) could claim any mechanical prowess beyond a simple prime and pull. But we all had Uncle Jack Quinlivan's phone number to resolve the inevitable contraption confusion. Yet, once you primed the tank, pulled the rope and had ignition, that machine became a raging powerhouse of snow-throwing. It was exhilarating (and a wee bit deafening) to direct that thing as the forward gear gave it the power to pull you over the snow as well as send plumes of the white stuff in whatever direction you could swing the metallic funnel that expelled it.

Snowfall has an immediate impact on travel, and certainly a dangerous one too for pedestrians when it arrives in relentless squalls. The ideal Christmas snow falls like the kind you see in snow globes; soft, pretty picturesque flurries. The precipitation referred to in Christmas songs is generally lighter than Lake Effect snow which drops thick, wet flakes that can easily clog a snow blower and stop a whole city's rush hour traffic in a matter of minutes. The snow that we children in the Northern Hemisphere pray for in mid-December serves the purpose of making the streets, home and businesses look prettier. It makes photographers and painters get ideas for next year's Christmas cards. It might close schools, too. But we also need to remember that God answers the prayers of those who need to navigate the white stuff to get where they want to be for Christmas. A praying driver in a Christmas Snow would call for the opposite of road rage… let's call it intersection intercession!

The Scriptural references to snow that come to mind include the prophecy of Isaiah 1:18 "Come now, let us set things right, says the Lord: Though your sins be like scarlet, they may become white as snow. (New American Bible)" And in the book of Daniel 3: 69-70, the song of the three youths "Frost and chill, bless the Lord. Ice and snow, bless the Lord; praise and exult Him above all forever!" (NAB) In places where winter gets fierce, it might be smart to sew these verses inside our insulated gloves or print them on scarves should we have to deal with wind chill factors and white-out blizzards on a regular basis. Shivering people will turn to God and say: "Let us p-p-p-pray!"

In this place of prayer, mangering our hearts
Find the stable, inside we go
Snow melts quick beside the fire
Word incarnate comes to show
Though we feel out of place, and flurried pulses race
One glance from Christ and the soul finds light
With the offering we're bringing,
can't help but join the singing
It's He whose praise the angels lift to Glory's height!

Looking For The Child

I'm looking for the child
Who once had simple trust
Who wanted to know God
And seeking, knew we must
Keep searching for the child
For whom angels would sing
One the night sweet Mary bore
Our Savior, Lord and King

There's grace for every child
So follow and adore
Repent and yet proclaim
His Mercy that restores
Who is your Christmas child?
Is hope stirred up within?
That this feast of His birth
Be the best that's ever been

Now bow before that child
Who makes us born anew
Profound simplicity
Transforming me and you
Our chance to be a child
Gives faith a deeper "Yes!"
Accept His saving love
With child-like holiness

We're looking for the child...

Monsignor Leo McCarthy came to live with me in the rectory at Blessed Sacrament Parish, Tonawanda when he retired. It would be hard to prove that he actually retired, when his energy level far exceeds mine and his involvement in Cardinal O'Hara High School where he's a chaplain could easily earn him time and a half for overtime. Instead, he's happy to serve, offer a priestly presence in the school, and assist the coaches in a number of sports. All of his 55 plus years of being a diocesan priest, Fr. Leo has had an ability to connect with young people. My cousins knew and loved him back in the late 1950s at my home parish of St. Teresa's. Those "kids" from that generation and every successive generation have been blessed by his ministry.

At daily Mass when Fr. Leo concludes the general intercessions, he uses a formula that comes to mind when I think of Advent and Christmas. He very often says something like: "We bring these prayers before you, Lord, with child-like simplicity and trust." We know that Jesus says we should seek the Kingdom of Heaven like a little child. Advent and Christmas have to be the time of year when most of us either get nostalgic for our Christmases past or tap into some of the excitement kids often have for that time of year.

For those of us who value being "grown up," a child-like part of us can still be developed and preserved. Not every family or home are places where a child feels safe and protected, but having experienced that in my childhood home, I consider it a great blessing. The innocence of youth quite often has a natural optimism and openness to dreaming. The imaginative minds of children remind us of the importance of playtime in our lives. Not competition but play, the kind of fun that comes through games where it doesn't really matter who wins or loses. In the best scenarios, the winners are those who laugh the most.

Parents might expend much energy toward finding out what toy or game a boy or girl wants for Christmas. If you can sit through Saturday morning cartoons or animated holiday specials, the commercials will all tell you that this particular item is the one that your child needs. Casual questions, cleverly masked in vague interest might find that your son or daughter has made a note to ask Santa Claus for one gift as their first choice. And then, with the best-laid plans of retailers and men, tiny children often have more fun playing with the cardboard box in which the toy came. Imagination can turn a simple box into a fort, a treehouse, a railroad train car, or a chapel. (Okay, not ALL of us played that way. If you did, chances are you're ordained. See if you recall this conversation in your child-like simplicity: "C'mon, let's pretend we're having a Holy Hour. Who wants to swing the incense?!")

In my first book there were a few stories shared of my childhood to illustrate how the faith of a child can also make one seem...naive. A number of readers shared that one of their favorites was the story of little Billy Q tossing a dead sparrow in the air, so that it would fly away before my Dad buried it. I don't need to look for that child, because he never left!!

Our looking for the child in Advent leads us with the shepherds and kings to the Holy Family, the birthplace of Jesus. In parallel, a child-like approach to preparation for Christmas can help generosity overcome pragmatism. Does someone need the gift that might cost a bit more? Perhaps not. Would they be thrilled, surprised and overjoyed as a little kid? If that's a strong maybe, a child-like playfulness in shopping or wrapping adds some fun to grown-up life and restores the kid inside of us to his or her proper place: humble yourself and become like a child.

Charities that benefit children don't usually struggle to find generous donors during this season of giving. Churches often have giving trees, and throughout Advent individuals or families take an ornament-shaped piece of paper that suggests clothing size or age of the recipient. While I join that majority in knowing the fun of shopping for children's gifts, some of us have to buy the 2X sweatpants for that little one's Mom or Dad. Perhaps the task of gift-giving for a child in need helps us connect more personally to the infant in the manger. But grown-up kids have need, too.

The arrival of my nieces and nephews began in 1984, and Christmas took a giant leap into kid-gifting. Although your children and grandkids, dear reader, are undoubtedly brilliant, I have yet to see a six-month old baby react to a Christmas toy with much more than a drool. That's okay, because for the first few children we need to be trained in shopping for those things that get the best reaction on their little faces.

I took great joy in buying tiny outfits for the kids. Children's clothing designers are wise enough to make little suits with tiny bow ties attached. And the dresses for a one-year old are cuter than you ever imagined. There's a good chance that I never even looked at the price tags when buying little dresses for Katie, Caitlin, Bekah and Grace. I was just glad I didn't have to try to put the outfits on them.

With numerous aunts and uncles on both sides of the family, sometimes there were multiple gifts of baby/toddler clothing. Nature provided for that, as the drool, baby vomit and food stains necessitated more costume changes on Christmas Eve than Cher or Celine Dion do in their Las Vegas shows. This way, baby gets to wear ***everybody's*** gift. Smart move on the parents' part, don't you agree??

Whether people know it or not, the season of Advent is a holy hunting season. The deer do not need to shudder at the thought of that. And we don't need to climb up a tree in the forest to wait for the "catch." The Lord God really takes the role of the hunter, the seeker. We are the prey, or rather the pray-ers He seeks. If we find something childlike in ourselves, if our imagination and memory take us back, our maker also wants us back. He invites, waits, baits (in a loving, gracious sense, not setting a trap!) and waits some more.

The child of God Our Father who is Jesus Christ, born of Mary and conceived by the Holy Spirit is alive and well when we celebrate His birth. We don't pretend that He wasn't born two thousand years ago, but we re-enter that mystery. The church attendance increase at Christmas has many aspects.

As a priest and pastor, my response to that has changed over the years. A turning point came when I was preparing a talk on Jesus for a parish renewal program called *Mission.* My visual image was a series of greeting cards. The Christmas card, at one time creating a giant, annual surge in US Postal Service volume was the first card that I showed. Hand drawn with crayon and marker, it drew a few smiles from the audience. We've probably all made them!

"The Christmas card Jesus" as I called Him, "has to be the most approachable image for sinners," I said. The baby Jesus cannot talk yet, and therefore, when we picture Christ as a newborn, our natural response is to approach without fear. None of the Infancy narratives in Luke's or Matthew's gospels say that tiny Jesus pointed at a shepherd and accused him of stealing a sheep from his neighbor's field. He doesn't sarcastically say to them: "Couldn't you have washed your face and hands before coming to my birthplace?" Not at all. Purely approachable and sweet, that Baby Jesus.

Parishioners who regularly attend church often find Christmas Mass a challenge. Not only is someone possibly taking their regular pew or parking space, but the crowd can make things quite chaotic. Lines for the rest rooms? Even the men's room? Now that is different from our usual practice. How do people greet the "Christmas and Easter" visitors? That differs, depending on their mood. As St. John Vianney reportedly used to say quietly as he heard twelve to fifteen hours of confessions in Ars, : "Me, too!"

How would a child welcome the stranger? At a certain point in their development, they do begin to act fearful of people they don't know. (Remember, I once worked as a children's portrait photographer. I've seen that terrified look.) So my recommendation to myself and the rest of us would be to greet them like a pre-teething toddler who smiles easily, drools often, and lights up with joy when you speak to them. Big smiles, all gums, not a clue…but warmly welcoming.

Okay, we all may have some work to do there. But don't run to your dentist and have all your teeth pulled, it's just an illustration. Be like a child, a happy child, a welcoming child. And the child who grew up to die for us will be most pleased. And the Kingdom that He came to preach will break through just a bit more. Look no more for a child. It's you, me… it's us!

Blanket of Stars

Blanket of Stars
Wrap the whole world this Christmas
Surround us, near and far
In God's woven Blanket of Stars

Comfort us in need of healing
Swaddle them with hope
Tuck us gently into bed with peace
Cover fear and hatred,
Like the night of Jesus' birth
Sleep safe under a Blanket of Stars

Blanket of Stars
Did you shine that first Christmas?
When the brightest one by far
Led the shepherds and kings

Cradle us in confidence
That from our mother's womb
God has knit us, His work of art
Rock our anxious worries
To rest in God's own peace
Underneath a Blanket of Stars

Over two millennia
We've looked to find this child
Holding fast to His word, His promise
Seeking to be witnesses
To God's most holy night…
Embraced in a Blanket of Stars!

Once while participating in a priests' retreat in Sioux Falls, South Dakota, I walked outside at night and looked up. "Where did they get all these stars?" I asked, kiddingly. In the city where I've spent most of my life, various forms of artificial light make it easier to navigate streets and recognize with the help of neon that a store is open or closed. But we forget that our view of the sky, the stars, and planets gets short-changed on a clear night. On clear nights we can see the moon just fine, but when that orbiting piece of God's handiwork is full, I also see the effect it has on people! Loony tunes and lunar light certainly make life more unpredictable.

I couldn't help but think of Abraham being told that his descendants would be as countless as the stars of the sky. Prairie skies look as though somebody took a giant bowl of diamonds of various sizes and scattered them into the stratosphere. It's overwhelmingly beautiful, and it surely added a sense of prayerful wonder to that retreat week.

When we picture the sky over Bethlehem on the night our Savior was born, we might fast-forward to the special guiding star. The reason our Christmas trees often have a star atop their peak serves to remind us of Heaven's newest star that special night. There are scientific theories proposing that several planets aligned to make it appear that a new star was shining. When we remember the sky over the manger scene, most of us don't get tangled up in explanations.

As the year 2000 approached, I composed my lyric and melody for *Blanket of Stars*. Perhaps my focus on the whole span of stellar points in space was informed by my years singing in choirs and my high school musical position upstage, near the back wall where tall people stood in the chorus. We who were surrounding the "shining star" were also part of the production. Even if you sometimes got referred to as "other" or "everybody else."

The image of the night sky as a blanket wrapping the earth makes sense. When we sing Christmas songs about sleeping in Heavenly peace it seems that winter beds require a warm blanket. And for parents, the subtle ballet of trying to tire out the children enough on December 24th to get their Christmas surprises in place. When sugar crystals as numerous as the stars find their way into the little ones' blood streams, a hyper-kinetic energy level that seems impossible to wear out results. Christmas cookie, anyone? Expect to be up late, Mom and Dad.

It does seem fair and right that the star of Bethlehem gets special attention. Whether it demands the spotlight or not, it *becomes* a spotlight. So all is calm, all is light. And Jesus forever will hold the title of Christmas superstar…so even a special star over the little town has to accept its role and give glory to the child in the manger. That means everyone in Christmas plays a *supporting* role, no matter how many lines they have. The ***true*** star is glorified by our "support."

One of my dear friends refers to my *Blanket of Stars* as "your lullaby." While it's meant to be lilting and soothing, my hope was never to put the listener to sleep! The song was originally recorded with the Voices of Mercy for our *Light of the World* album, and I later re-recorded it for the my first solo Christmas collection as the title song. But my very favorite performance of it took place my second Christmas as pastor.

Michael Rajczak was the 8th grade teacher at Blessed Sacrament Parish in Tonawanda. A talented writer, he also used to create an original Christmas play each year, featuring the class that hoped to graduate six months later. Skits were written to highlight the personalities of his class, with carols and hymns then included the rest of the school. I approached him after my first experience of his productions, and mentioned that I would love to collaborate and teach a few of my songs to the children for the next year. The collaboration ended up being more of a Christmas grand finale of sorts. Little did we know that 2007 would be the last Christmas before the school was closed.

We taught one of the younger classes my song *Blanket of Stars*, and they picked it up very well. I was very moved by the sound of kids singing this particular piece, as it seemed to be naturally a great fit for their voices. I don't know if I'll ever forget the tingle up my spine when they really began to sing it with feeling. And it's a good thing I had told them that I would start them out for rehearsal purposes and my voice would then drop out, because I am as sentimental as anyone and a sucker for Christmas "cute." It seems that a tear or two landed on the piano keys as I played.

A favorite scripture of mine is Psalm 139:13: "You knit me in my mother's womb." The same Lord who made the stars also has a purpose and plan for each one of His children. Reference to the Holy Spirit as Comforter also blends into the God-work of a blanket to cover us, warm us, and wrap us in His love.

BLUE BQ CHRISTMAS

I'm remembering a story that my parents used to tell about me when I was a toddler. Like Linus in *Peanuts*, many youngsters get emotionally attached to a blanket. For a brief time, I was told, I used to find my little blue blanket and announce that I was ready for bed. The "blue blankee" story opens me up to sibling teasing every time it's told, but my defensive response is that I was mature enough to know when it was time for bed. Security and familiarity are concepts that can also be woven into our love for Christmas traditions.

After I decided to call my first Christmas CD *Blanket of Stars*, I realized that a promotional item could help people associate the album's title with its namesake. I searched online, and found some very small children's blankets, but they were a printed pattern of same-shaped stars, more cartoonish than astronomical. These featured drawn five-pointed stars, but my Bethlehem sky concept needed more realism.

I approached the ladies of the parish who had begun a prayer shawl ministry, and discovered that a few of them were skilled at making quilts. I returned to shopping online, this time for cloth/material instead of a finished product, and was delighted to find a gorgeous material printed with a deep, dark night sky covered with stars. I ordered it from a place near Los Angeles, which made these blankets something like Hollywood productions!

We gave away most of the star-blankets in local stores that carried my CD, but I saved one for myself. After all, I paid for the blanket material which was a rich, dark blue. What 48-year-old singing priest would want to be without a "blue blankee" of his own? Actually, I use it exclusively for decoration, ***not*** bedtime, and hang it on a wall behind my manger scene with the addition of a lovely gold Christmas star. It's the one, after all that "led the shepherds and kings." This shepherd of souls has to give props where they're deserved!

A Manger Prayer

By the time she rested her head,
in Bethlehem, "house of bread,"
Did she sense salvation's dawning had begun?
With her child in purest light, with sweet Joseph in her sight
Could she see what this night of stable-birth had done?
    And so she prayed…
        "Father Almighty, Holy Great God
        True to your promises of old
          Protect my dear family and this baby in my arms
          He's your Son, as earth and Heaven now behold!"

Sees her donkey lying still, with no sense of Heaven's thrill
Just exhausted from his trek into this town
Did he care, carrying our Queen,
he'd have a place in every manger scene
That near-by was the Prince of Peace, come down?
    And Joseph prayed…
        "Loving Lord of Israel, pondering I praise
        as life begins again for all this night
        kindly king of providence, awesome are your ways
        I pray, with cattle lowing, to your heights!"

We look back to Christmas night,
faith still calls for deep insight
Like the Holy Family hearing angels' news
Flock of Christ, a fertile field,
still the world needs to be healed

Such good news for all, for many if we choose!
Now the Church sings:
"Faithful Lord of covenants,
hear our manger prayer
How can we but lift your name and sing?
Swaddle us within your love
Jesus Christ is born!
May all embrace the grace that He can bring"

Father almighty....Loving Lord of Israel...
Faithful God of covenants...Hear our manger prayer!

Should I ever find the time to write a third version of the classic science fiction film *The Incredible Shrinking Man* (1957) and its later spin-off, *The Incredible Shrinking Woman* (1981), *The Incredible Shrinking Priest* would find a tiny version of the lead character on Christmas Eve walking (or, better—leaping!?!) into a small tabletop manger scene. It would be fun, for a moment or two, to stand among the statues of shepherds and gaze on the ceramic Christ child. But then, one living person among all those little works of art would probably end in frustration. I wonder what the protocol would be? Would I be expected to stand still when others are looking, so as not to interrupt their prayer? Or could a very tiny voice offer a short homily, or at the very least the not-so-subtle suggestion that they pop one of my Christmas CDs into the stereo system to add to the moment?

Maybe I could write an *Aladdin Christmas Special*, where somebody gets three Christmas wishes, and they have to rub the jar of myrrh to get the genie out? No, that wouldn't work, and besides it would surely distract from the three gifts brought by the Wise Guys. Then there's my idea for a documentary-style pseudo reality show "*Bethlehem's Stall—*

the Unseen Footage!" Of course, implausibility would ***forestall*** that concept since there were no video or movie cameras two thousand years ago. And if there were, who would be so bold as to record such a holy night? Before every cell phone had a camera in it people actually experienced things, right?

So the St. Ignatius of Loyola style of prayer might be the closest thing to all these concepts, to "enter" the scene through prayer and "live in it" for a while. To engage the gift of imagination, one might try to see the flickering light of St. Joseph's lantern, smell the hay (and/or animals with questionable states of cleanliness…stables are not hypo-allergenic or antiseptic!) and hear the sighs of the child Jesus.

In my prayer the reflective heart of the Virgin Mary would have the most unique perspective on what has recently happened, after giving birth and finally sitting back to ponder it all. A modern Christmas card that I love depicts her asleep while St. Joseph holds the baby. But in my imagination she is usually cradling and gently rocking the Son of God. Because it's my imagination, she also hums to him. And because my mind tends to be on the lookout for ways to promote my music, she even hums ***my*** song. Hey—nothing is impossible with God, right??

Back to the manger prayer… as Our Lady reflects on the mystery that the Archangel Gabriel revealed, her bonding with the newborn child would have to be some kind of internal" reality check." The prophecy of a Messiah that she knew since her own childhood faith-formative years is now enfleshed, born of her virgin womb and resting in her arms. Talk about an eternal "wow" moment! It's no wonder that so much religious art tends to depict the mother and son. And years before that sacred spot would be embroiled in what feels like an eternal tug-of-war by factions and competition, this special moment of take-a-look-around for the Blessed Virgin seems more important to picture in our minds than the violent realities regularly being reported.

I turn our attention to St. Joseph in the song's second verse, and, for some reason, I picture him glancing over at the beast of burden that assisted in the Nazareth-to-Bethlehem journey. As we gaze around our churches during Christmas liturgies, we also wonder what unspoken prayers are being offered. Of course, there's also the reality that some family members attending church at Christmas are not exactly motivated by religious fervor but more by a desire to keep peace in the family. Thank God there are still clans whose tradition begins with worship of the one whose birth gives us the most important reason to celebrate. So, even if they have been led to church like the donkey that carried Christ's Mother, we all gather in His presence and are thereby blessed.

Admittedly, my penchant for puns in this song lyric could temporarily interrupt your prayer. Then again, the element of surprise in the playful "cattle lowing, to your heights" might just grab your attention. This is also meant to be a wink, an acknowledging nod to the classic *Away in a Manger*'s phrase: "the cattle are lowing." Personally, I've never heard cattle lowing. But now I have the idea to record this song (*A Manger Prayer*) and mix in either some actual cattle sounds or write a deep bass or baritone descant that ever-so-respectfully sings "mooooo…"

LET ST. JOSEPH SING!

And Joseph prayed… the bridge-line connects the descriptive/narrative verses with the refrains which change voices from the Mother of God to St. Joseph and, finally, to all of us in the final verse. As I said earlier, the post-birth and quietly bonding Jesus and Mary seems like a sweet thing to imagine. What, then, would St. Joseph's prayer be? In this song, he praises his Lord as the "kindly king of providence," camped out in the stall of a manger with his wife, newborn baby, and an assortment of animals. At least, in our compact home versions of manger scenes. I've read that the representative creatures of "all creation" may not have been so close by. If they were bounced out of their own stalls by visitors, the mooing would have to have a bit of grumbling mixed in. We presume that they had a sense of the importance of this night. Have you ever seen your cat or dog stay focused on any religious art when the sound of their food hits the feeding dish? Probably not.

The third verse intends to wrap us all into the scene. The flock of Christ gets described as a "fertile field," so the story of Christmas keeps calling us to an awareness of the ongoing faith walk. I'll admit that at certain points during the days of preparation I have muttered something to the effect of praying to get through Christmas in one piece, or to survive. But my hope, as a member of that fertile field (as well as a shepherd) is not to miss the opportunity for profound growth a holy Christmas season offers. Instead of "making it through" Christmas, can we rephrase our goal to letting each Christmas "make us"?

At Christmas liturgies we come to adore Him, and in about an hour we are sent out again, formally dismissed. Whether we are daily Mass folks or Christmas and Easter Catholics/Christians, or one-time visitors, the encounter's grace comes from the Lord Himself. Think of the number of scripture stories where people meet Jesus in situations that sound like a one-time interaction. Miracles happen, hearts are changed, burdens lifted, the dead are raised.

Let us also remember that those who choose not to join our congregations need Him just as much as we do. In the Word of God, the Holy Family eventually packs up and leaves Bethlehem's stall. Let's pray that the seeds of every Christmas get scattered generously, sown in our words, actions, and attitudes like the Word in Christ's parable of the Sower and the Seed (Matthew 13:13-23).

Some seed falls on those who attend, some get planted in the presider, the choir, and other ministers. And then our experience of Christ is to be taken out to the world. We become the sowers of the Good News. Maybe we should have asked Santa Claus for a new seed-spreader! On second thought, the Lord would say: "You don't need that—***you*** are my instruments!" Take that idea home to your family Christmas celebration this year.

Wrapped

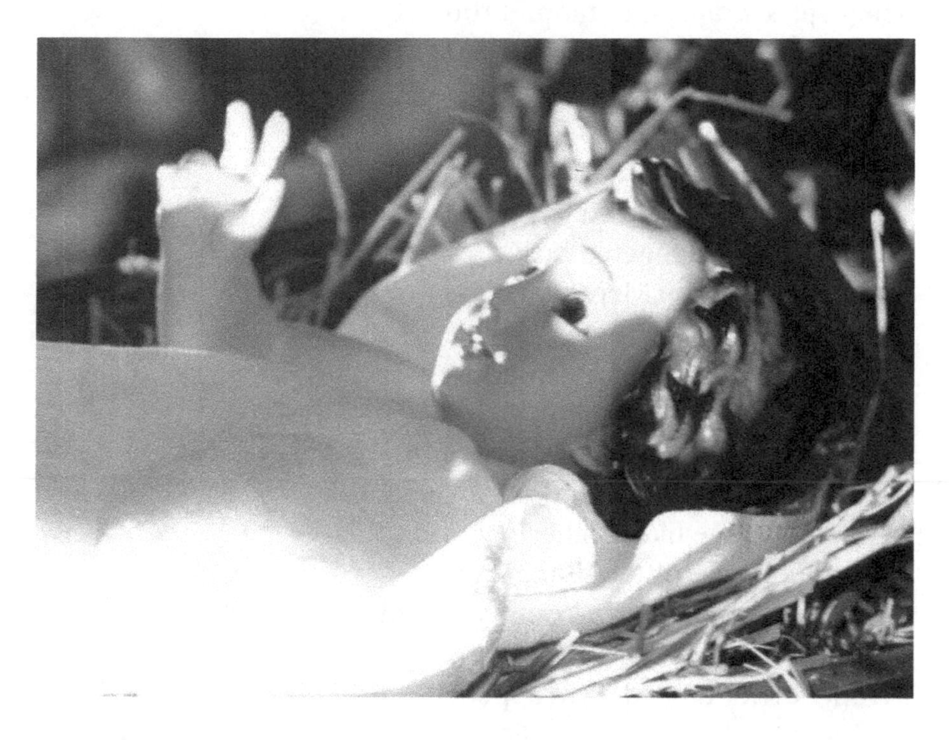

Wrapped in swaddling clothes, prefect gift of Christmas night
Newborn Jesus in her arms, angels soaring in the heights
When the love of God came down,
bands of cloth embraced Him tight
Soon His arms would reach to us,
gently turn our wrongs to right!

Wrapped in travelling clothes, off to Egypt, taking flight
Trusting Providence, they'd go,
world in darkness hates the light!

But in family's embrace, ev'ry migrant finds a home
Fleet of foot but firm in faith,
never from the Father's will to roam!

Then He's wrapped in rabbi's robes,
yet not held by laws that bind
His heart loves to hug the lost,
breaking in new kingdom-kind
Every word He spoke gave life,
swaddled sinners, saved by grace
Jesus, Mary's mangered boy…
show His Father's Mercy face!

Now we're wrapped, if we choose to be,
like a mountain of Christmas gifts
Let Him share all that you have, give the holy poor a lift!
Love of Christ wraps neighbor's need,
warm and close like mother's womb
We're the Body of the living Lord,
who left wrappings in an empty tomb!

Wrapped….wrapped….wrapped!!

Most people probably cannot remember the experience of being swaddled as a newborn. The tradition goes way back to wrap a baby rather snugly in an attempt to mimic the close quarters of the mother's womb. The scriptures say that Jesus was wrapped in swaddling clothes and laid in a manger. In my Christmas prayer and reflection, it struck me that this one verse is something I've come to take for granted. Then I found a connection between swaddling clothes and the wrapping of the gifts that we give. *Voila!* A song was born. And I wrapped it in a simple melody that has a lullaby-like feel. (So I hope that you read the lyrics of my song aloud, or you may just fall asleep and miss the rest of this chapter!)

The awesome mystery and miracle of the incarnation can be seen as the Son of God *wrapped* in flesh. And it can be extended to the image St. Paul gives us, that in baptism we "put on Christ." In a deep spiritual reality, the grace that our Lord gives in salvation *more than* wraps us. It claims every cell in our body and invites us to give Him the gift of obedience to His will. We are, then, profoundly bonded. (But you, know, *Bonded* would not make such a nice song title—it sounds like a dental procedure, so I'll stay with *Wrapped*!)

The environment around a just-born baby has to feel dramatically different. Arms and legs and head movement tend to be squishy and floppy with as-yet un-developed muscle control. But babies tend to revert to what they call the "fetal position" with legs and arms literally almost wrapped around its own torso. Swaddling imitates that closeness.

The first verse of my song sets the tone for the foreshadowing that Christ's birth offers us. The hands that are so tiny, the arms that will someday reach out and touch, heal the sick and embrace the frightened and lost sheep who are now still in baby form. And just as there might be a few layers of soft cloth used to swaddle, layers of *meaning* invite our prayer and meditation at the wonder of Christ's birth.

People who have experienced Arctic cold need to be familiar with methods of layering clothing in the dead of winter. When wind chills go into double-digits below zero degrees Fahrenheit, Long John is no longer the priest known for his lengthy homilies but a thermal swaddling method for warmth. Babies are only swaddled for a short time, but the need for winter blankets and comforters and such bring me back to Bethlehem. Especially a few times during power outages when I suddenly realized that a back-up generator would have been a good thing to put on my letter to Santa Claus!

FLY LIKE AN EGYPTIAN?

My *Wrapped* lyric attempts a wide-view whole-lifespan look at Jesus Christ. From swaddling clothes we move to the event of the Holy Family's flight to Egypt. While many families have members who pack up suitcases and travel to gather at Christmas, that time of year is never ideal for a move! (I know that from experience. At one parish where I lived, a new rectory was being built when I arrived. The pastor and housekeeping staff chose December 27th to move the three priests and whole house. Ah—so memorable, so cold! But at least we took comfort that, un-like Jesus, Mary, and Joseph no Egyptian Pharaoh was pursuing us in our flight.)

Have you ever imagined what the trek to Egypt looked like, assisted by the religious art that gives us a glimpse? With nothing but that faithful donkey and a whole lot of faith in God, St. Joseph and his spouse took the most precious gift humanity had ever been given through a desert, to save His life. I only went through a desert once, and being a winter-loving northerner, it was traumatic.

On one hand, the photographer in me was astonished at the beautiful colors in Arizona on a drive with some friends from California to Utah. We were in a rented van, and I was appropriately soaked in sun screen. As a person of Irish descent trained to avoid direct sunlight, I leaned casually toward the shadiest spots in our seats and pretended to be calm.

About two or three hours into the trip, we started seeing desert—and lots of it. Then, suddenly a sign from the highway department appeared reading: "Turn off Air Conditioners or Cars Will Over-Heat!"

My sun-loving friends were very calm, but I immediately protested: "Hey! No one warned me about THIS!!" We rolled down the windows soon after that, because deserts can warm up a momentarily cooled van very quickly and transform it into rolling microwave ovens. The hot wind just kept getting hotter. I've endured a lot of blizzards and low wind-chill factors in my life, but I'd kiss a frosted car windshield before I would ever drive through a desert again.

Do you realize what I just did? Wrapped myself in a self-pity party merely because modern conveniences were temporarily denied. Shameful, I know. Spoiled, I admit. So, now as I try to picture the Holy Family walking/riding a donkey through Egyptian sands, winds, and heat my admiration for them multiplies. Add to that the fact that there was no way to make a reservation at the Cairo Hilton. And then, the inevitable thought: will there be room at any inns there? Is God taking them on another faith-testing camping trip with His Son? To our amazement, they had enough trust in God to follow wherever He led. Let's remember that Advent can be a desert-like time, while Christmas is a get-on-the-road and travel time. Are we and our families wrapped in a similar faith? We have perfect examples to follow.

RABBI WRAP?

As the song lyric moves through the life of Christ, we come to an image of Jesus wearing the traditional garb of a rabbi. His disciples called Him "teacher" and "rabbi," and we know that He spoke to/argued with the Scribes and Pharisees often. The third verse of my song refers to the irony of St.

Paul's concept of freedom in reference to law. I situated that within a phrase about law being binding, as swaddling clothes bind a baby. Jesus fulfilled the law and sometimes reached beyond it to touch and heal the poor, the sick, and even to raise the dead. He taught with authority, yet He was a constant source of challenge to those who argued in favor of traditions that, in the end, were more human than divine. In a sense, Christ's life and ministry within the Jewish tradition were similar to those updates we need to install in our computers and smart phones. He was God's gift to them first, actually.

There's also the concept that our Lord and Savior can "swaddle sinners" or keep them close to Him although our thoughts, words, and actions can separate. The ministry of Jesus, as well as the ministry of His Body the Church today, holds sinful humanity close like a crying baby needing the comfort of love more than the discipline of punishment.

How do you picture the face, the countenance of Jesus in the synagogue or preaching like a rabbi on the hillside? My firm conviction is that He "showed His Father's mercy face" which drew people of all types toward Him. Would you purchase a piece of religious art that tried to show Christ scowling or correcting someone in righteous anger? Straight to the budget bin with that one, I say, and I'd bet that a Christian retailer literally wouldn't be able to give it away.

It helps to remember that the one who was wrapped in swaddling clothes became ***our*** wrapper, the gently gathering shepherd. Despite our weakness and a list of faults that God could write in complete detail but mercifully keeps to Himself, try to imagine a pleasant look on the Lord's face when He looks at you, at us. The prophet Zephaniah (3:17) tells us that the expression is delight! Yes, baby Jesus can smile and coo, but grown-up Jesus has always been approachable. Maybe we've let others draw His image differently because of the way they believe Him to be more frightening than friendly. His mercy endures forever, and we simply need it for our whole lives. Wrap your head around that and you might just take a few quicker steps toward following more trustingly.

Bethlehem Boys

Bethlehem Boy, a manger your crib
Your nursery this holy night a stable
Bethlehem Boy, infant-sized
Let me bow before you while I'm able
While Joseph tried to find a room
You slept within the purest womb
I travel back to days of old
With one request; be it so bold
Now that you're born, what would be the harm
If I could hold sweet Jesus in my arms?

Bethlehem Boys, innocent ones
The rage of a tyrant caused your dying
Bethlehem Boys, martyrs so small
A terrified crescendo of crying
As waves of grief tsunamied all
Your swaddling clothes turned funeral pall
In victimhood, your witnesses arise
As humankind keeps falling before your eyes.
Let us not forget, we are not far from there
As un-planned parents need our fervent prayer

Bethlehem boy—my, how you've grown
Your little town of birth remembers proudly
Carpentry past, seeds you have sown
But crowds you healed and fed protested loudly
When the holy child became a man

Your saving truth revealed God's plan
From manger wood to glorious cross
You lived and died that none be lost
This Christmas let your sorrows turn to joy
by the grace of our dear Savior, our Bethlehem Boy.
Praise Jesus Christ, our Bethlehem Boy!

In the Scriptures people refer to Christ as Jesus of Nazareth. That place is the subject of the question "Can anything good come from Nazareth?" (John 1:46) And Bethlehem is given the distinction in Micah 5:1 of being called "too small to be among the clans of Judah." It seems like our Lord was purposely supposed to be from places on earth that were insignificant. Then, as His identity and mission became known, God would be glorified more.

In this lyric I have nicknamed Jesus "Bethlehem Boy." In South Buffalo where I grew up, many people were given nicknames. The culture had a tendency to do that, normally as a term of endearment. My referring to the Lord as Bethlehem Boy was meant to bring attention to the slaughter of the Holy Innocents by King Herod's murderous rampage. December 28th, just three days after the joyous feast, we commemorate the innocent children who were lost. (The day after Christmas is also the feast of St. Stephen, the first or proto-martyr who was stoned to death. Are the liturgists kill-joys?? No. Think of it more as carefully placed celebrations to remind us how much the world needed the Savior. And we still do, don't we? Read your newspaper on Christmas Day and see that violence, hatred and war are still keeping Herod's bad example alive.)

The city of David, Bethlehem, means *house of bread.* Ever since I've learned that, I love the symbolism of the newly-born Christ child placed in a feeding trough or manger.

And we can easily see how He came to become the Bread of Life, not manna that falls from the heavens but the incarnate Son of God who would die for our salvation. Scientists call a pre-born human child a *fetus*. From Latin, it means "little one." And this little one whose birth calls for our attention will feed us like nothing else in the universe, with His own Body, Blood, Soul and Divinity. It's the banquet of life, the Holy Eucharist!

SONS OF OTHER MOTHERS

My friend Father Richard McAlear, OMI gives a beautiful talk about our Lady at the time of Christ's birth. When he speaks of the Holy Innocents, he shares the very earthly, practical reality that the mothers in Bethlehem would have interacted. As there were no laundromats, and especially for Mary and Joseph, no friends or relatives, (otherwise, they would have had a room on that awesome night!), the diaper washing would have taken place at the nearest river or creek. And since babies have similar patterns of eating and sleeping, it is conceivable that all the new mothers in town for the census would be together in their duties.

So when the singular Bethlehem Boy in verse one becomes Boys in the second stanza, the song truly puts flesh on the bones of the story we've heard in the Bible. I always imagined that St. Joseph and his holy wife heard about the innocents later on, and were horrified at the massacre. But when you picture the Virgin Mother might have actually known the names of the other women (and, possibly, some of the children), it raises the compassion to a much more personal sorrow.

As an ordained presbyter and preacher, the memorial of the Holy Innocents always stirs me to prayerfully intercede for those who are planning to end the life of a child in the womb. No matter whether man-made laws call it a "right" or "legal," in God's eyes it has to extend the cries raised for the Bethlehem Boys. The death of a child has always seemed like one of the deepest wounds a human heart can experience. In Matthew 2:16-18, the fury of Herod is unleashed on all boys two years old and under. In our times, the tragic "choice" continues to take human lives while still growing and developing inside their mother-even to the ninth month of pregnancy. We must never stop working to bring this practice under the false guise of "medical care" to an end. Distancing ourselves from it would be like hearing the news of the slaughtered Bethlehem Boys and then moving on with our day. It's important to see ourselves connected in the human family, as the Blessed Mother is to the mothers of the victims of Bethlehem's death brigade.

FROM WOOD TO WOOD

The baby Jesus grew into adulthood and left home. His journey began in Bethlehem then took Him to Egypt as the flight of the Holy Family saved Him from the sword. From Egypt they eventually returned to Nazareth until His public life/ministry began. From the wooden manger of the stall where animals fed to the hill of Calvary where He was nailed to wood, this Bethlehem Boy had quite a life.

I wonder where the wood came from that built that manger. I also cannot help but ponder how many times Jesus heard the sound of nails pounded into wood at the home where he lived with the carpenter. And then, as he apprenticed and built objects of wood Himself, that common everyday material was familiar. Finally, the victory over sin and death, as He was put to death on a tree and rose triumphantly three days later!

No matter what our life's sorrows may be, or our world's headlines that echo the Bethlehem Boys in the modern day Herod's terrorist attacks, Christ's amazing grace remains available to us. Ultimately, that Bethlehem Boy came to save and that is what He does (and always did) best! At Christmas we can swaddle ourselves in that for comfort and joy!

Gloria

Did we hear an angel choir, on this night,
on our watch on this hill
In our hearts, a strange new fire,
laying eyes on that child, what a thrill!
Are we shepherds now or sheep?
In this joy there is need to be led
How in Heaven can we sleep, angelic song still in our heads!

Gloria, Christ is born, worth the wait, Love breaks through
Mystery… veil is torn…best good news…now…we're new!!

Can we learn the angel hymn? Join the chorus, being one
So profound, no moment's whim
To know what His birth had begun
Christmas calls us to take stock,
work to bring His peace to Earth
Look around, for we form the flock
of the shepherd who'll teach our worth!

Gloria! Dark meets light, sin and death, He'll defeat
Melody… marks the night, angels sing, we….repeat!!

Who can live the angel song? Make the choice,
find your voice, give a gift
Why not come and sing along?
He deserves all the praise we can lift!
Bethlehem still makes us see,

Every year, ev'ryone can reply
Bow our heads and bend the knee,
find the will to really try…

Gloria !!!

In the moments after the shepherds of Bethlehem experienced the angels revealing what God had done, did you ever wonder if they turned to each other and asked: "Did that *really* just happen?" And which one of them was the first to follow through and head into the city to look for a baby lying in a feeding trough?

The Scriptures don't give a full account of what they said on their way, or whether they muttered anything to St. Joseph and the Blessed Mother. How does one explain to a stranger that God sent an angelic messenger who was accompanied by a choir of Heaven's angels singing "*Glory to God in the Highest and Peace to His People on Earth*"? Of course, the couple they visited in the manger stall would have very much been able to relate. For both of them had received messages, guidance, and good news. Not everyone gets such a privilege, and I imagine the shepherds were more than a little self-conscious approaching and trying to justify breaking into this tender family moment.

But God's glory is like that. It keeps encouraging us to move closer to the Lord, whether a glorious light or an experience of the glory of life's most beautiful moments. My lyric for *Gloria* takes up the shepherds as they depart the site of Christ's birth. If they thought that angelic choirs in the sky were awesome, we can hardly imagine their reaction to having seen the Son of God soon after his birth.

When we compare these simple men of the Bethlehem fields to the magi or kings of Epiphany, these working-class folks represent everyone who feels drawn to Christ at Christmas. With no gifts to present, the shepherds had to be quite a sight. Religious art depicts them as kneeling, even standing a bit outside of the entrance to the place where the savior had just been born.

Speechlessness would be perfectly understandable. But there had to be awe and wonder on their faces, joy and delight when they realized that they were not hallucinating or dreaming in their field that night. The duty of the shepherds at that time of evening would be simply to watch and protect the flock from predators or criminal-minded thieves. None of them could have envisioned what this day would bring. A life-changing, world-saving breakthrough from the maker of Heaven and Earth!

So my lyric gives them some Holy Spirit fire, a burning in their hearts more than thirty years before people would hear Jesus preach and sense something divine. The transformative night could have easily led them to the question my song proposes: "Are we shepherds now or sheep?" having encountered the Good Shepherd Himself! How could they even begin to know how to process this glorious moment in history?

If there were a way to measure an adrenaline rush, the one felt by the field workers of Bethlehem had to be off the charts, as we say. Simply going back to their duties, one of them picking up a flute, another throwing another log on the watch fire, is hard to picture. And the song from the hosts of angels? Don't you wish you could hear it? The very first Christmas carol, or better—the singing of the first Gloria that we proclaim in song at Masses on Sundays and solemnities! The melody had to be continuing to echo in their heads like any catchy song we hear. (As the kind of melodies we songwriters *hope* to compose!)

I see this scene as a prefiguring of Pentecost. Holy fire in their hearts, and although we do not know how close they came when they saw the child, could the newborn Jesus have "breathed on them"? At what point did they decide to depart from the scene of glory? How long did they stay? We do not know, but it's exciting to imagine it. Did one shepherd suggest that it would be good to let this woman who just gave birth have a little rest?

The second verse of my song switches the focus to us at Christmas. The song of glory and the very reason the angels appeared connects us to the coming of Christmas. We're invited to learn the most profound and inspired song (in our

his Good News spreading.
into a timeless chorus of
host. Angels sing Gloria,
in memorization, so our
in our souls.
an angel who has to be
Holy Family. She carries a
ria in Excelsis Deo. (It
e figures I arrange in the
que. I have what I call
sons depicted. In fact we
t seems they almost equal
y one angel.
manger scene: Gloria, as
wing. For about twenty
drop have been carefully
g has a picce of strapping
for packaging) that holds
aloft and silently singing
t see her broken wing. It
ter fit together just right,
front. Of course, Christ
ture. So my friend Gloria
le who hear her song and
join it.

YOUR MOST AWESOME GIFT?

Have you ever received a Christmas gift that took you completely by surprise and totally surprised and overwhelmed you? The world received the perfect gift of the Heavenly Father in His only Son. No one can ever top that! And, thanks be to God, we cannot even try to out-do the Lord. My first Christmas as a priest, one of my classmates surprised the rest of us. Fr. Dan Young had written to Mother Teresa of Calcutta and asked her to pray for the group of us.

At Christmas, he gave me a framed postcard with a personal message from the holy saint of Calcutta, complete with a signature! I was flabbergasted at receiving this gift and blurted out: "This is one Christmas gift that will be *hard to top*!" Now that Mother Teresa has been canonized a saint in the Catholic Church, this note card is a relic. All I know is that when I try to imagine the response of the shepherds as they walked (or ran!?) out to start telling people what they had witnessed, I've had a taste of such a holy surprise.

Kings and Things

When most people assemble their Nativity scenes, it's a depiction that's something like the grand finale of a Broadway musical, or the final bows. The entire cast of characters appears at once, even if they never shared the stage for a scene. Newborn Jesus, of course, deserves eternal curtain calls. The parental figures would be the next most important.

After the human beings get their accolades, I would surely give a standing ovation to the donkey who carried the Mother of God from Nazareth to the little town of Bethlehem. The beast of the holiest burden worked mighty hard. A mouthful of hay and bucket of water were probably his only paycheck. Now *there's* a humble actor!!

We may not think about the overlap of having both shepherds and the Magi/Three Kings present at the same time. No scripture ever mentions them meeting, nor showing up the same night. How embarrassing *that* would be for the lowly shepherds, as the others park their camels outside and offer their expensive gifts! Besides, the shepherd story comes from the Gospel of St. Luke, while the astrologers from the East are in St. Matthew's account.

Our family manger scene had only shepherds at the manger for Christmas. Not that we were scripture scholars, mind you. It's just that my parents liked to create a dramatic entrance for the kings. After all, Mom did attend Jane Keeler's Drama School in Buffalo back in the 1940's. (We never found a certificate of completion, but that was fine with us. Enough daily, or even hourly family drama was provided while raising six children who inherited her flair for the dramatic!)

Our figures for the Magi were un-wrapped from the shoebox full of crumpled newspaper and paper towels the same day as the rest of the people, angels and animals. But they were placed on a little shelf atop one of our archways to create a tangible distance for their trek. After Christmas came, in the days between the celebration of the birth of Our Lord and Epiphany, we moved the kings a little bit each day. Come Epiphany, they were standing right there among the Holy Family and miscellaneous animals. A solitary camel (we may have had three at one point, but, again, with six kids—and statuettes break easily) with his tired legs folded underneath him gave a symbolic gesture to match our post-Christmas exhaustion.

The combination of St. Luke's shepherds and St. Matthew's magi make for a winning combination, so don't fret about having them crowded into your manger. The shepherds stand for the simple and the nearby, while the visitors from the East represent the far-from-simple as well as the far-from Bethlehem. Christ's mission was to save all, so our approach to a Christmas crèche doesn't require showing identification as a member of the Actor's Equity Union. Coming to Christ humbled by our need for a savior gains us an audience with the Lord who was manger-born.

Besides the oh-so-familiar classic *We Three Kings*, I'd bet that many Christmas carolers would be hard-pressed to sing two or three more hymns from memory that specifically accompany this feast. When I realized that, one year, praying in my rectory chapel, I composed a lyric that would eventually become a new song. The star of Bethlehem had always been a source of fascination to me, so why not sing about it? A star-song is born!

HEAVEN'S SHINING LIGHT

Come, you wealth of nations
Burdened as they carry
Jewels, crowns in darkness
Strapped to dromedary...
Come, prepare to worship
One you've yet to see
Homage due by instinct
Soon, they'll bend the knee!

How deep shall we bow?
Which riches do we bring?
Treasures here are nothing
For the infant King

Awash in His Glory, over Bethlehem shone
A super-star pointing, that Christ would be known
Stand under its guidance, this life-changing night
Hand of God revealing... Heaven's Shining Light!

Come, you proud and selfish
Spare no precious stone
Value what's eternal
Forget Herod's throne!
Give yourself to Jesus,
recognize your Lord
By His saving grace
You'll see your lives restored.

How deep dwells His love, as fear evaporates
One star points to Him as Good News becomes great!

Awash in His Glory, over Bethlehem shone
A super-star pointing, that Christ would be known
Stand under its guidance, this life-changing night
Hand of God revealing…Heaven's Shining Light!

Ouch Be Home For Christmas

In the popular imagination, the coming of Christmas always goes well with the classic literature title *Great Expectations* as much as *A Christmas Carol*. The build-up becomes very often more than most feasts/holidays can achieve. And, though it's considered impolite to say that Christmas is a disappointment, isn't that a very common experience?

Pop culture and the treasury of music for the season seems to sugar coat the whole thing, and that just adds to the danger of our celebration becoming superficial. We don't need to sprinkle sugar over everything. Instead, we need to adjust our expectations to include first and foremost the religious meaning of Christmas: Jesus saves, He doesn't disappoint.

Children might whine if they didn't get the toys that caused a riot the morning after Thanksgiving, or the computer game that costs as much as his grandfather spent on his wife's engagement ring. How obvious can it be that we need to teach the kids that it's not merely about gifts? It can include that, but only in connection to the mystery of the Incarnation. Can we ever say that God disappointed us by sending the gift of His Son? Hardly! We can also honestly admit that for too many of us, our overflowing calendars from December 1st through the 25th get so heavy that there's no room for Christ except for an hour in church. When that's the case, don't we give God more reason to be disappointed *with us* than vice versa?

Every life has its up and down cycles of events, planned and unplanned, that are awesome in joyous surprise and most painful in tragedy. And without sounding like a pessimist (realist says it better, I guess) we will all have bad, sad and painful experiences at Christmas at some point in our lives. No egg nog additive or mistletoe moment can instantly heal a truly broken heart. And that's okay, because it simply reminds us that our broken human nature is precisely what Jesus Christ came to lift up, to save by grace and redeem.

Probably the most agonizing Christmas for me was 2004. The year had included amazing and wonderful things. Early that August I had the chance to sing at a priests' retreat in Dublin, Ireland. But less than two weeks later, my brother Joe's 13-year-old son died as a result of an accident. There are no words to describe the loss of a child, and although I was only Jimmy's uncle, it was probably the most tragic death I had been close to. Nobody would wish it on their worst enemy.

So, Christmas arrived, ready or not, about four months later. I was always, as I may have repeatedly mentioned in this book, a life-long Christmas junkie. Some people save that kind of enthusiasm for their favorite sports teams, but for me, my Super Bowl/World Series/Kentucky Derby win has been Advent into Christmas. Each year, preparing for my homily at Christmas Masses, I usually have written a new song. Some years, when my imagination perks (and the coffee flows while I'm composing) there are two or three new songs.

But that Christmas, I was stuck. Dread describes it best. I worked hard to get out of the Lord's way, praying for some musical inspiration to lift my preaching into something meaningful and singable. But my writer's block was an iceberg. So I sat down and tried to put what my heart was feeling into a non-traditional lyric for a Fr. Bill Quinlivan song.

Uncomfortable Christmas was born slowly, through tears and anguish, praying in the perpetual Eucharistic Adoration Chapel of St. Gregory the Great Parish in Williamsville where I was assigned at the time. I remember thinking as I wrote it: "Nobody is ***ever*** going to want to hear this song! We'd have to distribute anti-depressants after Mass." I could hear the congregations chant "Father Scrooge, Father Scrooge!!" Or frowning parents with toddlers at the door afterwards: "Thanks a LOT Father Bill. You really bummed *us all* out!"

In the twelve years since that December, I rarely went back to that journal again when searching for songs to complete. In fact, the brown leather book where this lyric was scribbled was never even filled. I know that is very impractical of me and not at all environmentally-conscious to waste that paper. Sorry, friends—some things you just cannot re-visit for a while.

In the beginning stages of planning this book, a box of my old journals was pulled out. I vaguely remembered several unfinished Advent and Christmas lyrics and homily ideas so I wanted to salvage them. So, as you might guess, old brown leather Book of Bummer was there. I decided to find the lyric because I believe that the Lord used the power of words to help heal me. Even though I couldn't bear to read it for almost a decade afterwards, something told me that it needed to be included. Finally, I re-read and prayed with the text and brought it to completion.

The reflective process in re-reading my journals helped me see that a "bummer" Christmas song was not necessarily something that would ruin other people's holiday. Instead, it could become a vehicle to reach the shattered hearts of people whose saddest, toughest year might be this Christmas. It might be best illustrated as a person hearing *O, Come All Ye Faithful* while under their breath, in a brutally honest whisper responding: "And then ***get me through*** Christmas as ***fast as possible***!!"

The lyric at this chapter's start has had some polish applied. At first, it just kind of ended after a litany of phrases about why Christmas makes our struggling seasons worse. But I realized that the kind of joy that's stolen can often begin to heal with one's eyes focused with laser precision on Jesus. Remember, He doesn't disappoint. Yet at some moments in our life we need Emmanuel, God-with -us for comfort. Even though we have no desire whatsoever to rejoice.

I read somewhere a profoundly simple definition of compassion: shared passion. That's probably what we need to seek in our grief and sorrow and our losses. Isn't that why grief support groups help so many people? Of course, everyone grieves differently, so there's no magic formula. Just like Christmas really isn't a "magic" time of year, in the sense that magic is merely illusion. Christ's coming to earth has a reality beyond our limited minds, and His compassion points us with our crosses to resurrection.

The more I think about it, that's why I began a practice of calling people on Christmas Eve who've suffered a loss since the last celebration of that holy day. It wasn't until my family went through it that I could be more aware of how difficult the season will be for someone every Christmas. Now, don't worry--that will not keep me from my newly-restored Christmas zeal. It just reminds me to balance out the ho-ho-ho with the ***oh-oh-oh***.

UNCOMFORTABLE (BUMMER) CHRISTMAS

Lord, come carry my family through Christmas
Disconnected from comfort and joy
As I smile through the tears, looking busy
And still somehow rejoice in your Boy
Who was born and would share in our sorrow
He has pow'r to lift boulders of pain
Shepherd us through this grief-stricken snowstorm
Burdens weigh me down, like Marley's chains…
It's more than blue, absence all-too-true
Feeling numb to their holiday glee..
There's a too-empty place
One less beloved face
Most uncomfortable Christmas, you see?
Perhaps I'll learn compassion this Christmas
As I block out the carols and bells
Now aware of how many souls suffer
Find their hearts at the bottom of wells…
It would all be in vain but for Jesus
Who turns anxious self-pity to calm
I've no strength for much more than the simple
Christ is good news, pour myrrh's healing balm!
Can people tell that I hurt like hell?
A "little Christmas" is more than I need
Family's gaping hole, dressed up bleeding souls
Most uncomfortable Christmas, indeed!
To focus on our Savior is the most important task
Come, light our deepest darkness, in your love let us bask!

As church bells peal, we begin to heal
Broken ones, make some room for His Peace.
Like the shepherds, kneel,
Son of God, you're REAL
This day's not about us, it's your feast!!

Mercy At Christmas

Your Mercy sent the angels
It calmed the shepherds' fright
Helped Joseph find a birthplace
A shelter from the night

There's Mercy born at Bethlehem
It's God whose reach is long
It's calling everyone to sing
A Christmas Mercy song!

To let us embrace the Good News
And with the Virgin, God's will to choose
We'll know the presence of Mercy at Christmas

To fill human hearts with a sweet-joy song
He came and absolved all our sin and wrong
Right from the first there was Mercy at Christmas!

If we want Peace on the earth to begin
We can't tell God there's "No room at the inn"
Born is the gift of Mercy at Christmas!

If we can just turn from our selfish ways
Seek holy virtue, spend time in praise
We'll find ourselves wrapped in Jesus this Christmas!!

Your Mercy sent the angels…

About ten years into my involvement at St. Luke's Mission of Mercy, two strongly connected strains in my heart found themselves woven or, better, braided as one. For most of my priesthood, God's mercy (which St. Faustina Kowalska's Diary, *Divine Mercy in My Soul* describes as His "greatest attribute") has seemed to drive and enhance my calling; my personal need for it as well as my desire to proclaim it.

An Advent Penance service is the obvious place where we might usually associate Divine Mercy and Christmas (my *other* great strain of devotion!) Various not-for-profit organizations have come to rely on the holidays as a season of giving. Food banks, soup kitchens and other charities will concur that people are generous at Christmas time. Catholic parishes don't ignore this fact, either.

The works of mercy, of course, are meant to be yearlong and life-long expressions of our faith, not something we put away with the Christmas decorations until the next time around. Because God's mercy comes offered too often to humanity, we can be grateful that it's perennial—actually, eternal!

One day while I was at prayer, it dawned on me that none of the Christmas songs I had written ever clearly connected mercy with the feast of the Lord's birth. I challenged myself to marry the two (some cultures still have arranged marriages- and apparently they often work out!) Marrying them in my mind had to simply take two great loves of my heart (not persons, but concepts…) and introduce them, seat them at my piano together, if you will and let love bring them together.

Let me propose a visual for these two great things intertwined. Actually, the design of a traditional candy cane will do nicely. The red and white are associated with the rays of mercy flowing from Christ's pierced side in the image of Divine Mercy. The shape of candy canes is said to represent a shepherd's staff, Bethlehem's field full of shepherds, or the Good Shepherd Himself! So Christmas and mercy make a sweet concoction, don't you agree?

In one sense, the mercy of God harmonizes well with Divine Providence. Our Lord provides for us mercifully, generously, and continually. So my lyric gives credit and glory to God's mercy for sending the angels, calming the shepherds, guiding the holy couple (still with child) to a birthing place, and while we say that the Word and love became flesh, we can extend that to mercy being born at Bethlehem.

From the very start, we can see the mercy of God all over the story of Christ's coming as our savior and king. And His mission to reconcile and save all creation would supernaturally then also be "***mercifying***" (a word coined by Pope Francis for the Jubilee Year of Mercy) by His presence. When the timeless stepped into time, the world's transformation by His grace begins. Therefore, at Christmas we can already glorify His mercy as he "Came and absolved all our sin and wrong." Our common experience of absolution in the sacrament of penance continues the mercy-gift that was born of the Virgin Mary.

MERRY CHRIST- MESS?

Recently, I read a commentary on Luke 16:19-31 (the story of the rich man and Lazarus, the beggar, not the brother of Martha and Mary). It said that when we try to create a "perfect world" for ourselves, we inherently feel the need to eliminate people whose presence makes us uncomfortable. The messy aspects of our fallen humanity might cause a scrupulosity that leads us to believe we must not interact with other sinners for fear of contamination. God's mercy doesn't instantly perfect us…we keep striving for it, although we still have faults and failings. And seeking His mercy gives us reason to praise the Lord; it's not to send us into despair but to encourage us to keep coming back to His grace.

Looking at the infancy narratives in both Luke and Matthew's gospels, we quickly find that the Lord sends His only-begotten Son right into our mess. Crazed Herod is soon out to kill the newborn king, even manipulating the magi for his own evil intent. Smelly shepherds, unschooled in the ways of the world are probably wiser than the Scribes and Pharisees with their noses buried in their scrolls. What is God really teaching us when simple animal herders look to the sky and see angelic heavenly messengers? What better use is there for astrology than to point these star-students to the same manger? Christ Jesus is the ultimate route-changer, with a way to the best destination in the universe!

An Advent or Christmas without seeking the mercy of our Lord in confession simply cannot be as joyful. Our internal disorder caused by sin can use some serious heart-housekeeping to set us back on the path to glory. Cleaning obsessed people and "neat freaks" might panic when wrapping paper ends up all over the floor at a large family's gift exchange. Tables of snack foods might look like a sprinkling rite of peanuts and popcorn took place. But mercy undoes the messy. Our God brings all things back into order when we obey Him.

Remember that the Lord didn't zap Caesar to change his mind when he had the idea for a census, though it would make little towns like Bethlehem a little bit of bedlam for a while. He didn't even give Herod amnesia when the magi came before him to be sent on a mission based on fear and a dastardly plan to destroy the baby king. God doesn't force Himself on anyone, though the draw of His love and grace has a "force" to it---always freeing, binding us to God and each other; not as chains of slavery but with wings to fly.

In the text of Mary's Magnificat, her "spirit rejoices in God my savior..." (Luke 1:47) and she joyfully proclaims "His mercy is from generation to generation to those that fear him." (1:50) Every generation needs the mercy that our Lord pours out, and there is an ongoing invitation to receive it, rejoice in it, and then proclaim it to others.

Every Advent and Christmas, mercy makes us merry. Like Mary!

Silent Might

At the first glimpse of Jesus, we wondered
Did He know we had waited so long?
That the Father was writing a melody
Word enfleshed, whose whole life was a song
As the first angel chorus proclaimed it
Did they realize -God made a choice
To reveal Heaven's power in an infant
For which carols still join, ev'ry voice

So in awe he spoke not, good St. Joseph
Humming sweetly, Our Lady wrapped Him tight
Jesus, comfort and joy born at Christmas
Smiling, swaddled Son of God...
Silent Might!

Can we travel in prayer to the manger
To the night of "No room at the inn"?
Hold our tongues, in amazement we witness
The beginning of the end of our sin
But tonight we continue to know Him
As God's infinite Love came so small
Somehow, dumbfounded, yet we're adoring
Holy baby who will save one and all...

So in awe, he spoke not, good St. Joseph...

Seek some deep quiet pray'r time this Christmas
Take a moment, contemplate His worth
Put to rest noise and all loud distraction
Let us take a "pregnant pause" at His birth!

So in awe, he spoke not, good St. Joseph...
Silent Might!

When Advent concludes and the first Mass of Christmas begins, we need to be aware of the spiritual transition, as if a piece of music modulates up a whole step. Should our internal eye, our hearts and souls' focus go up half a step (which is one key on a piano) or a whole (two keys) or more? Evaluate your Advent season for a few moments to see whether you were able to find some quality time in reflective prayer. Don't give in to the temptation to begin by feeling guilty for having a "busy" time. Instead, pray to the Holy Spirit to be grateful for the fruits of your labors in prayer and meditation. After all, those are the things you carry into church when you arrive for Christmas liturgy. There's no need to try to wrap gifts prettier, or mask the fact that it was an "impulse buy." We all know this type of purchase. The items placed in racks at the check-out counter that are meant to entice us to pop a few more things into our shopping cart!

Take comfort in the fact that Jesus waits for us throughout Advent. His patience, knowledge and wisdom are perfect. Any hint or wide swatch of perfectionism within us must eventually be put aside when accepting God's invitation. There's no commandment to have a perfect Advent season, but a gentle, persistent invitation and encouragement to offer the Lord some space in each day. The expression "spend some time" might help us if we empty out our credit union

Christmas Club account to buy gifts. How much ***time*** do we budget for Christ?

Good news always has the potential to become great news in the Lord. If your Advent went bust by the second day of trying to read that little prayer booklet your church handed out on the Solemnity of Christ Our King, it's not too late to change gears. I imagine that faith-filled people in every parish where I've served can start Advent by marking their Bible for the Scripture readings for the First Sunday of the season, then find (in the blink of an eye) that it's the last day of the fourth Week of Advent and the bookmark never moved and the pages did not get read. The Lord appreciates the best laid Advent plans of *Church Mice and Men*!

So—here's some really good news: we can take advantage of the ***season*** of Christmas. A priest friend of mine doesn't send his Christmas cards in time for December 25th but takes some quiet time in the days afterward so as to be more focused and relaxed. One year I decided to send Epiphany cards; even bought some with no pine trees or manger but only the Magi up front. But at the last minute, my Irish guilt won out and they were mailed "in time." A few years later I discovered at the after-Christmas half-off sale some lovely cards featuring an Advent wreath. Bought several boxes, thinking that I could sign and write any time during the four-week season. But as I recall, they were in the mail at my regular, habitual time as I crossed the task off my list of things "to do."

Concepts such as this take time to apply. One family that I know raised their children to never expect more than three gifts from Santa Claus or the family. Their rationale was heroic: since Scripture and tradition tell of Jesus receiving gold, frankincense and myrrh, what makes you think you deserve more than three, more than ***He***? (Have I followed their fine example? Not yet. My dog still gets several more presents than the Wise Men brought to Bethlehem. But I continue to be inspired by the idea with hope that I could someday try it!)

WHAT DID HE SAY?

My lyric for *Silent Might* entertains the question of what one might hear upon visiting the scene of the birth of the Messiah. It's laced with irony, for no one would reasonable expect a newborn to speak. But in the silence, in the quiet, in the holy presence of Our Lord, wasn't the gift of His very life already speaking figuratively, to all creation? The word became flesh, and before a discernable word in Aramaic (the vernacular at the time and place of Nazareth, we're told) would be pronounced, the Heavenly Father was speaking and showing forth His love by sending His Son. Jesus would grow and learn to speak—and His disciples would treasure His words!

As a musician, I tend to musicalize things, so the mystery of the Annunciation where the angel reveals God's plan to the Virgin Mary is like a prelude or an overture. As my song says "word made flesh, whose whole life was a song," the living word has the power being poured out like melody. So music raises a sentence or phrase and infuses it with life. The might of God as the plan of salvation enfolds, the same power that split the Red Sea and calmed the storm calls us to sacred silence. It's the very reason why lectors and proclaimers of the scripture, as well as preachers leave some silence at the end of important sentences. I always say when training lectors: let it echo out across the church, to work its way into people's hearts. And if the windows of the church are open- highly unlikely at Advent or Christmas Masses in Buffalo New York- the image of the Word continuing to go out to all creation can be worth meditation.

Because St. Joseph has no quoted words in the Gospels, I assigned him the non-speaking role of awe-filled baby Jesus holder in the refrain. My version of the Blessed Mother would be something like my own Mom who was a constant (though almost unconscious, by habit) hummer. So I see her "humming sweetly" to the tiny baby savior. Babies respond to music, and have heard it while they're carried in the womb. When children get older, they might take on the role of music critic and suggest that instead of singing their Mom simply mouth the words to a song playing on the radio. Of course, Jesus would never do this to His precious mother. There were no radios yet! And as she was the Holy Mother of God, let's show some respect here!

The Son of God seems best pictured to be smiling as He is swaddled, wrapped and held close to the heart of His mother. But we all know that babies don't always have smiles on their faces. Believe me, I worked as a portrait photographer for a year, and the younger the baby, the more difficult it was to have them smile on demand.

The deep, sacred sleep of a tiny infant can elicit a touch of envy from people who experience frequent insomnia. For a just-fed, just-diaper-changed little one, their sleep becomes heavenly peace not only for them but for their parents/babysitters. When we imagine approaching the stable as visitors, some of us might be a bit nervous based on our "don't wake the baby" life experiences that a sleeping child startled from its slumber can cause. High volume sounds from those tiny lungs one might not believe to be possible. Some crying babies seem like the kid was a descendant of Broadway legend Ethel Merman whose lung power could produce sounds a Bose speaker would admire!

After I baptize a baby, I like to ask if I can hold the child when the ceremony is over. My uncle training comes right back as I instinctively start to rock back and forth. Cradling a newborn in your arms, you almost don't want to set them down or hand them off to the next person waiting for a snuggle. (With the baby, not the priest!) Should their expression change to a grimace and their cheeks get red in preparation for a scream, I can pass them back faster than an NFL Super Bowl quarterback!

Priesthood's Epiphany

With hearts like Magi gold
Priests bow before their King
Then full vocation bloom
Epiphany will bring

Wise men adore Him,
Rest in His gaze
Giver of all gifts,
receive our praise
Breathe in His Spirit
Come, bend the knee
With three gifts of
Priesthood's Epiphany

Lives burn sweet frankincense
Prayers rise, intercede
Uniting all who serve
Up, billow all our needs

Wise men adore Him...

Lord, myrrh these listening souls
Ourselves to sacrifice
To be what you anoint
We feed the world with Christ

Wise men adore Him.......

In comparison to the astrologers who followed the star and found Joseph, Mary and the baby lying in the manger, our journey with Christ includes breakthrough moments we might call "epiphanies." The first inkling of a new opportunity to grow in faith has that sense of standing on a ledge, being invited to dive into uncharted waters. In our zeal we may not pause to consider whether we ever learned to swim. For the call of our God always provides, and in spiritual matters, we're probably never completely prepared. If that were true, why would we need trust or faith?

A vocational call to serve the church as a priest can be so mysterious and rather difficult to discern. It's as if the process of preparation, seeking one affirmative answer has two Bethlehem stars; one in the heavens, another in the heart/soul of the one called. And from my experience, I can share that it's usually one or the other, and not too often both shining at the same time. When the sense of purpose and being led is strong and clear, those epiphanies are cause for a major feast in themselves!

In this reflection I want to focus on ordained Catholic priesthood in the context of the epiphany of the Lord. Our Eastern Rite sisters and brothers refer to this feast as the Theophany, a Greek work which means "manifestation of God." The traditional date is January 6th, and actually long before Christmas appeared on calendars as December 25th, this divine mystery was considered an essential Christian feast. The finding/discovery of the newborn Jesus by people other than the Virgin Mary and St. Joseph symbolized a breakthrough. (With apologies to the shepherds of Luke's Gospel, here Matthew's infancy narrative apparently had greater effect in liturgical calendar and date setting!)

We refer to our priests as shepherds, and encourage their ministry to be humble. On Christmas Eve they serve "flocks by night" as midnight nears. Yet, at the same time, our vestments and the placement of a presider at the end of a procession have an air of something royal. Of course, the king here happens to be Jesus Christ, whose priesthood, eternal and awesome, is shared with mere mortals. So, both priestly and kingly roles have meaning in pastoral work.

BOWER POWER

On the day of priestly ordination, the candidate for the sacrament of Holy Orders spends time lying face-down in prostration as the church gathered sings a Litany of Saints. From time to time, I still feel the need to pray in the prostrate position. It's a posture of total surrender, even powerlessness before God. It's as if you were having a humility oil change! (And I recommend, as the auto mechanics do when getting your car serviced, getting new air filters and the highest grade of oil!)

From my first years of being a Roman Catholic priest, I have valued the experience of praying with brother priests at Eucharistic holy hours. For almost twenty years, I have been part of a priestly fraternity called Jesus Caritas, inspired by Blessed Charles de Foucauld. Members of the fraternity put aside a day each month to spend as brothers. A shared meal, a confidential Review of Life, conversation and a holy hour are the essential elements.

There's a beautiful peace in that time of silent prayer in the presence of Jesus in the Most Blessed Sacrament. Part of the commitment of the priest-brothers is to intercede for one another throughout the month, and quietly adoring the Lord has a way of blessing the bond of fraternity. Each month, the individual priests are also asked to commit to a daily holy hour and what we call a Day in the Desert. These special prayer times in Advent have blessed me profoundly.

The desert days differ from a day off, where one might end up running errands and catching up on personal things like haircuts and dental appointments. A day of prayer, alone with the Lord, opens the heart, mind and soul to the voice of the Lord. Of course, we know that not everyone hears an audible voice, yet the time a priest spends in prayer acknowledges an openness to epiphanies that direct, encourage, renew, and correct our ways.

I have made a number of my annual retreats in Dublin at the Intercession for Priests in August. Every morning, there is a holy hour in the main chapel. When I lie prostrate on the cool stone floor or kneel or sit quietly, often I am inspired with ideas for new Christmas songs. These come like the gifts of the Magi, in various forms. Though not intended to sell enough CDs for a certified "gold record," some nuggets of concepts become treasures. As the clouds of incense linger in the chapel and lift with the priests' prayers, praise becomes a natural response. And the myrrh which the infant Jesus was given, which is also used at the time for preparing a body for burial, reminds me of the Sacred Chrism with which my hands were anointed for priestly ministry.

Have you ever wondered what a priest prays for? Beyond our best recollections of every request we receive throughout the day of "Father pray for me/ my family/job etc." a priest's pastoral role requires him to pray for his flock. There's even a law that requires him to celebrate Mass once per week *pro populo* (Latin) or for the people he serves. And the Liturgy of the Hours or breviary also helps remind him to intercede for his people while praising God through the Psalms.

The longer I live my calling to priesthood, the less apologetic I am about praying for myself. In a very personal way, a pastor must commune with the chief shepherd who is divine, listen for his master's voice and bow before the Almighty. With the help of their spiritual directors, priests must be aware of the call for their own ongoing conversion to the Gospel. Creeping self-centered attitudes and behaviors in the celibate life must be monitored conscientiously so that a priest might keep seeking to discover how to serve more effectively with the heart of Christ.

A mindful heart, a pondering spirit helps to not only remember what's on the list of appointments and meetings but to prayerfully look at the present and future of parish life for insights. I love to picture the shepherds in the Bethlehem fields like a gathering of priest brothers. At any given moment, was one of them expressing concern for a lost sheep, or perchance did any of them have an injured sheep on their shoulders when the glorious angel choir appeared? Were any of them having a "bad shepherd day"? (Believe me, very honest self-examination can bring to light truths about oneself that make a "bad hair day" look like a picnic!)

PRAY FOR YOUR SHEPHERDS

Do you pray for your priests, deacons, bishops or hierarchs at the Cardinal level, especially the Pope? When Pope Francis was introduced as the new Holy Father, his first request to the people of Rome and the world was for prayers. And he has consistently asked just about everyone who meets him also for prayers. If you've ever felt ill-equipped for your work, or role in a family, try to imagine being the Vicar of Christ on earth. That would find me face-down and begging for prayer faster than you can say "On your mark, get set, panic!"

During Advent, it is a wonderful to pray for the priest who will celebrate the Christmas Mass that you will attend, to lift up in prayer the clergyman who will hear your Advent confession. Let's not forget those aspiring to become ordained priests, our seminarians. December and Advent usually coincide with term paper and final exam stresses. And the members of a seminary formation team may be seriously considering asking a candidate to take some time off if the discernment is leading to that conclusion. Seminary professors surely appreciate our prayers, too.

In every parish community there is a percentage of people who put their priests on their Christmas card mailing list. Even if it includes one of those bragging letters or a photo album of grandchildren's pictures, it's a touching gesture. I honestly don't recall my parents ever sending a card to our priests at the home parish. I'm more than a little embarrassed to admit this, as I have been the recipient of not only a number of sweet cards but also the special-buy "Merry Christmas to Our Priest" variety. It amazes me every time to realize that people search the card rack to find such a specialized card and send it to me.

What gift does a priest offer to the Lord and His people at Advent/Christmas? Yes, we can send out a massive mailing with a stamped signature…when we care enough to send the very convenient! Or we can dig deeper, and return to the image of the Magi in my *Priesthood's Epiphany* lyric. The traditional three gifts of gold, frankincense and myrrh can be given by a priest in his daily living out the promises of obedience and celibacy, and in his personal and public prayer. The gift that can be described as "good as gold" is that of our undivided attention given to those who approach us at the church door or call the parish office seeking a private appointment.

Epiphanies still happen in my priesthood, often while observing someone else living with generous hearts in marriage, the single life, religious orders or priestly life. We all have the gift of Jesus who, with the Father and Spirit, is ever-faithful to us. And the gift goes on.

This Is Christmas

There's a tendency to sugar-coat the story of His birth
Like a children's tale or mere civil holiday its' worth
It's tempting to be, sometimes, superficial on this day
Simply mark a feast, miss the meaning
O people let me say…

Beyond party themes…this is Christmas
There is faith above food and fun
Besides lights and trees…there's the manger
For God came to Earth…in His Son!

You hear "Have a happy holiday" or
"Come by for a drink"
You see lawns dressed like the Vegas strip
But where, where's the Jesus link??
We should run our Christmas calendar by the Lord;
Say: "What do YOU think?"

Between Christ and us, bridging distance
In your heart and hearth, let Him in!
Dare to welcome Him, He's no stranger…
He loves all our friends, and our kin.

Let the scripture come alive until you hear the angel chorus
Here we worship that same savior
and He NEVER will ignore us

As we celebrate this holy time, let Him increase believin'
Praise your King, become His servant
Find a joy that's never leavin'….

Among those who know Holy Christmas
There's great mystery and we're blessed
But He sends us out like the shepherds
Such good news, Christ is born, go profess!!
This… is… Christmas!

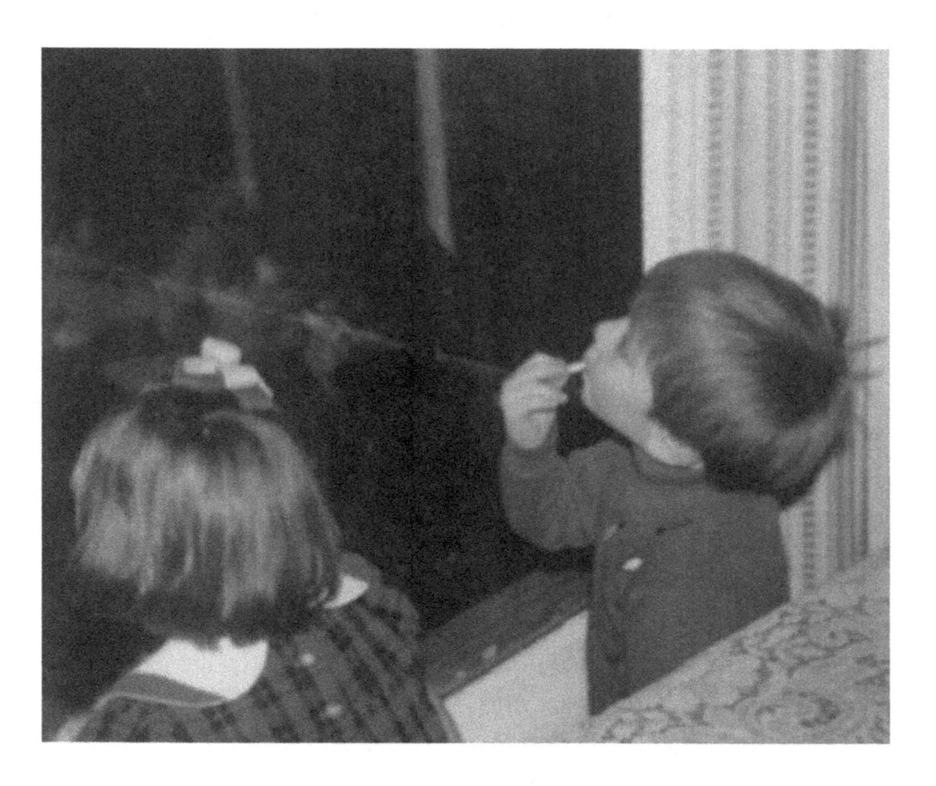

When the glorious feast of the Incarnation comes each year, have you noticed that the secular celebration can drown out our voices? Several years ago, I gave my parishioners at Blessed Sacrament parish "homework" one Advent weekend.

They were to take an hour, or at least half an hour and listen to one of the twenty-four hour Christmas radio stations. Keeping a scratch pad nearby, they were assigned to count the number of times a song actually referred to Jesus or His birth. Another scoring column was for snowmen and snow, one for reindeer, one for bells and another for romantic notions. If anyone in those mentioned Christ's birth, we might be surprised. But I knew going into this that a few secular radio stations included a fairly healthy mix of *Silent Night* and *Hark, the Herald Angels Sing*.

It ended up as quite an eye-opening exercise. Although the JPMs (in Christian radio they used to use that term for Jesus-Per-Minute mentions of the Holy Name) were significantly lower than the *All I Want For Christmas Is You* and *Baby, It's Cold Outside* repetitions, the Lord did get mentioned. So we reflected together the next weekend on the results. On one hand, a cynic/pessimist could say: "They practically ignore Christ's birth..." but the optimistic voices (like mine, sometimes… and I'm optimistic that this will *increase…*) can take solace in the fact that the holy was included. On December 26th when many of them used to switch immediate back to pop, country and rap, hip-hop and other types of music, the name of Jesus would not be heard in praise. In generations gone by, gospel songs might actually make it into the mix of a non-religious station if it is a great record. Those days seem long gone. But I find much joy in hearing "Christ the savior is born" in the mix. Didn't Jesus come to bring salvation to all?

So the observer of pop culture celebrates and accepts the inclusion of the religious theme as a positive. Of course, there's an occasional thematic clash when the playlist suddenly segues from what one might call a Christmas lust song to a traditional, solemn hymn where angels announce the birth of the Son of God. But evangelization doesn't usually produce new disciples from inside a germ-free bubble. So just as Christ was born in a rather less-than-sanitary space of a stable, His first words were not: "Ye filthy beasts…you DISGUST me!" We often find Jesus in the mix, especially within our own hearts. And we are called to live within that mix, too, in the world, yet fixing our eyes on the Kingdom.

FINDING AND KEEPING CHRIST IN CHRISTMAS

Many people like the bumper sticker than says "Keep Christ in Christmas." Of course, I do, too. But the slogan presumes that people have already found Christ. People cannot keep what they've yet to find! I like the one that says "Wise men still seek him" because seekers can be finders, and if we lock people outside the doors of our churches because they're not regulars, we have lost the point of the Gospel as good news. Even those of us in full-time ministry have to admit that the demands of energy and time in Advent and Christmas risk masking our soul's need to find and keep Christ in our personal, family, parish and wider world's celebrations. The finders must be keepers.

For several years, one of my priest friends who has the gift of frugality sent Christmas cards that, strangely, had no mention of Christ's birth at all, except a mix of "happy holidays" and cute snowmen and winter village scenes with no steeple (I always look because I grew up in a home where we could see our church steeple from the back yard!) I used to let it bother me. But my hope is that the grace of God has moved me beyond my frustration to write a lyric like the one that leads this chapter. The greeting of "happy holidays" does include non-Christian people, but if it becomes the singular greeting of believers, how do we witness to Christ in that moment?

Picture yourself standing at New York City's Grand Central Station at a peak rush hour. The noise and commotion are legendary. Then, see yourself whisper "Christ is born! Let us adore Him!" Some Catholics use that as a greeting from the Vigil of Christmas on the 24th of December through the Baptism of the Lord, also known as the liturgical Christmas season. Now, pray with hope that the people who lean in to hear you whisper the phrase begin to repeat it. No one yells, but the message is spread. How long would it take to get a great number of folks to join in? I don't know…over two-thousand years? We need to keep proclaiming Him until He comes again.

VOICES OF MERCHANDISE

For a number of years, I belonged to a music ministry at Buffalo's St. Luke's Mission of Mercy. We were called Voices of Mercy. About a year after we began singing together a woman approached us with a special request. She was the General Manager of a large department store in a suburb of Buffalo, and asked if we would come and sing in her store during a specific day of the Christmas shopping season. She added that this request was for the sake of the store clerks who had to deal with not only a high volume of sales but some very demanding customers. What self-respecting Christian music-maker could deny this request? "I want you to bring Jesus into my store for Christmas!"

We wondered whether corporate headquarters would approve of a religious group being invited to such an event, but it can safely be presumed that they were looking mostly at sales receipts and not musical content. We were impressed by this woman of faith who cared enough to infuse a presence of Jesus' name and His birth into her workplace!!

We gathered near an escalator in the center of the store, where there would be a lot of people coming and going. I believe we had about three guitars, perhaps a tambourine and/or sleigh bells. And about seven voices. We prayed together, then started to sing some of the most well-known hymns and carols. At first, people smiled politely as they rushed past. It could be that some of them saw my Roman collar and thought that the presence of a priest might indicate a collection?!?

After several songs, we noticed several people hovering near some racks of clothing. They stood at a distance, not rummaging through the winter coats on the rack but listening. We could see their lips moving, as they found the courage to quietly sing along. By the time our leader, Norm Paolini, Jr., the co-director of the Mission started quietly strumming the last line of verse one of Silent Night, I noticed that a number of people had tears streaming down their faces.

As experienced lay missionaries, instinctively several members of the group stepped out of our group formation and spoke with the shoppers, listening to stories of grief, heart break and pain. I realized that another reason why people rush past carolers is that the music being played or sung touches a very deep place in people's hearts and memories. I see it almost every Christmas at Masses, especially when we sing Silent Night. Something so profound happens with the sweet melody and simple yet inspiring words. (And I need to share that this classic was written by an Austrian Catholic priest, Rev. Josef Mohr and his organist, Franz Gruber. It was created quickly one Christmas when the pipe organ broke! Its first performance was accompanied by guitar only.)

Music brings up emotions and heals the spirit of people. And Christmas music has a deep hold in people's souls, like old folk songs, patriotic songs and school theme songs. When I look back on that sale at the mall, I don't recall purchasing a thing. But I can still see the strangers opening up, the lay missionaries smiling at them, hugging them among the marked-down winter coats.

And looking back on this kind of experience, I want to sing: THIS is Christmas!

Come Home to Christmas

It's like December flips its days until the 25th one
Despite a whole year to organize,
some plans simply won't get done
We'll arrive like tardy shepherds,
barely finding manger scenes
It's about the birth of Jesus,
so remember what that means

It's time to come home to Christmas
To the Lord who has called us His own
Fill the pews, raise our voices in worship,
Find new joy, let no one feel alone
It's familiar and sweet to be gathered
For there's room in this Bethlehem stall
Being shut out of inns, full of frenzy
In this child's heart, there's a place for us all.

Some spend this holy day in places
they would never choose to:
In hospital rooms and prison cells,
will those folks hear good news, too?
At missions where they shelter the poorest
Some deployed, others getting chemo
Let's hold them in our tender prayer to
Jesus Christ who, at His birth lets us know…

It's time to come home to Christmas
To the birthplace of comfort and joy
Aren't we led by the light of a new star
To bring gifts that sing hope in this boy
When the Word becomes flesh we start seeking
Ways to turn selfish hearts inside-out
Don't forget we're all family in Jesus
God is with us, let there be no doubt

Home, where the heart is.
Heart, where faith finds birth
Christmas always calls us back
To start living again Peace on Earth.
Welcome home, welcome home to Christmas!

Certainly, most people are familiar with the beloved song *I'll Be Home for Christmas*.

It's been long associated with the era in which it was first written and recorded, over 70 years ago, in 1943. (The well-known lyric was penned by Kim Gannon, music composed by Walter Kent and additional writing credit goes to Buck Ram.) The World War II generation has been associated with the song, and while it poignantly reflected the situation of soldiers who could be home "only in my dreams," it has also touched other people separated by miles at Christmas time.

In the decade after my graduation from college, I attempted to make my mark in the entertainment industry. I wrote a few scripts for television, did some comedy writing for show biz legend Joan Rivers and actually completed a screenplay for a television movie. The film title was *Home for Christmas*, and it was the story of a young woman who moved to Buffalo and found herself stranded by a huge snowstorm that cancelled her Christmas travel plans. I pictured the apartment where she lived being like a South Buffalo building at the corner of Seneca Street and Mineral Springs Road. Actually, my Uncle Bill had an apartment there for many years.

My idea for the conflict of the story was built around real-life experiences of lake effect snowstorms that regularly crippled our city and caused joyous un-planned school vacations for kids and teachers. After one of the most brutal storms I ever recall, I trudged down my street to Seneca, which was a main artery, and saw that the city had called in the National Guard to remove the several feet of accumulated snow. I ran home to get my camera, and shot a few images of that military activity, which was happening right at the intersection near my Uncle Bill Murray's apartment building, the setting for my fictional story.

Several years ago, an idea came to me to put a new twist on the *I'll Be Home for Christmas* title, and have a new song be about coming home *to* Christmas itself. And, by extension, then, it's really about being at home in the true meaning of the feast day. It's not about geographic location or familiar faces but our belonging to the family of God, the Church.

As a parish priest, I enjoy the experience of seeing people gather with family and friends for the liturgical celebration of Christmas. After spending a number of years in a parish church, priests who are blessed with good memories can learn the names of the family members who drive or fly in for a homecoming. With a memory like mine, one remembers faces. College students who live in dorms, near or far, return with a look of relief after a completed semester. I had that look myself for nine Christmases, looking back over my state college years and seminary formation time.

The home where my siblings and I grew up was the only house that most of us remember as home. If you had asked me in my youth to picture myself gathered with family in another place, it would be hard to conjure an image. The same living room and mostly the same furniture appear in family photos, appearing first in black and white shots of the early 1960s, and then lasting all the way to the days of digital photography. Since then, I have lived in a number of rectories. And virtually every member of the family, including Mom and Dad, who have each spent Christmas in very different places, hospitals and nursing facilities.

Home seems to be so much more about a state of mind than the physical place. While the first half of my life found me in the same house December 25th, the second half of my years have moved me about. We've even had different siblings host the big family get-together and gift exchange on Christmas Eve. And I've realized that home is made by loved ones, not brick and mortar.

CONCLUSION—BRINGING IT HOME

When I began to gather up ideas for this Advent/Christmas book, I went back through my prayer journals for many Decembers. I also read through my parish bulletin columns from Advent through Christmas to see if there were any ideas worth mining for publication. Some things were used. While I also realized that bulletin columns five years later don't always make much sense. That's okay, and it gives me empathy for those who still read my weekly writings.

My desire for this collection of song lyrics, stories and reflections is that people will start to think and pray more intentionally through both the Advent and Christmas seasons. In January 2016 I found myself in the early stages of preparation for writing while visiting my Irish friends in Florida. While praying before the Lord Jesus in Eucharistic Adoration, another idea occurred: to include an addendum in the back of the book, with prayers.

The ones I composed that day and in the months following attempt to bring you some spiritual focus and companionship through the always full weeks of Advent and Christmas. Perhaps you and your loved ones already have prayer traditions to surround and prepare you for the tasks of Advent and Christmas. If not, I'm delighted to be able to start you thinking of ways to praise the Lord whose birth gives the whole world reason to pause, reflect, and celebrate.

Christ is born. So come, let us adore Him and experience Christmas for its true meaning.

About the Author

Fr. Bill Quinlivan has recorded seven CDs of original songs, and this volume includes the back-stories of many of his compositions. Before becoming a priest, he was a comedy writer, aspiring screenwriter, and worked in radio. For a time he served as a portrait photographer as well as a stint as a government employee at the IRS. He now works for the "perfect boss." The BIG boss! Fr. Bill is the fourth-born Quinlivan, raised in predominately Irish Catholic South Buffalo. But his first fifty years have taken him to other corners of the world. He is currently pastor of St. Martin of Tours and St. Thomas Aquinas in South Buffalo, New York, in the Diocese of Buffalo. He was ordained in 1995, and in addition to his diocesan assignments is involved at St. Luke's Mission of Mercy on Buffalo's East Side, a ministry to the homeless and addicted.

Photo by Patrick McPartland